A Traveler's Companion
to North Dakota State Historic Sites

A Traveler's Companion
to North Dakota State Historic Sites
THIRD EDITION

STATE HISTORICAL SOCIETY OF NORTH DAKOTA
Merlan E. Paaverud, Jr., director

North Dakota Heritage Center, Bismarck, ND

2014

Front cover

Chateau de Morés, de Morés State Historic Site

Frontispiece

*Map of village sites on the Missouri River,
I-ki-ha-wa-he (Sitting Rabbit), Mandan, 1905*

Editor, first edition

J. Signe Snortland

Sites photographer and map designer

Brian R. Austin

Publications editor, third edition

Bonnie T. Johnson

Cover design

Brian R. Austin

Interior book design and typesetting

Judy Gilats

Printing

United Printing, Bismarck, 3K, September 2014

© State Historical Society of North Dakota

All rights reserved. Published 2014

Printed in the United States on acid-free paper

ISBN 978-1891419423

Library of Congress
Cataloging-in-Publication Data

   A traveler's companion to North Dakota state
   historic sites. Bismarck, ND: State Historical
   Society of North Dakota, 1996, 2002, 2014.
      216 p. : col. ill., col. maps; 23 cm.
   Includes endnotes and index.
   1. Historic sites—North Dakota—Guidebooks.
   2. North Dakota—Description and Travel.
   3. North Dakota—History.
   I. State Historical Society of North Dakota.

Contents

vii   Preface

viii   Foreword

ix   Visiting the Sites

1   Introduction to North Dakota's Past

5 HISTORIC SITES

6   Big Mound Battlefield State Historic Site

10   Bismarck-Deadwood Stage Trail State Historic Site

12   Brenner Crossing State Historic Site

13   Buffalo Creek State Historic Site

14   Camp Arnold State Historic Site

15   Camp Atchison State Historic Site

18   Camp Buell State Historic Site

19   Camp Corning State Historic Site

20   Camp Grant State Historic Site

21   Camp Hancock State Historic Site

24   Camp Kimball State Historic Site

25   Camp Sheardown State Historic Site

26   Camp Weiser State Historic Site

27   Camp Whitney State Historic Site

28   Cannonball Stage Station State Historic Site

30   Cross Ranch State Park

32   Crowley Flint Quarry State Historic Site

34   David Thompson State Historic Site

36   De Morés State Historic Site

40   Double Ditch Indian Village State Historic Site

44   Former Governors' Mansion State Historic Site

47   Fort Abercrombie State Historic Site

50   Fort Abraham Lincoln State Park

53   Fort Buford and the Missouri-Yellowstone Confluence Interpretive Center

57   Fort Clark Trading Post State Historic Site

62   Fort Dilts State Historic Site

65   Fort Mandan Overlook State Historic Site

67   Fort Ransom State Historic Site

69   Fort Rice State Historic Site

73   Fort Stevenson State Park

76   Fort Totten State Historic Site

81   Fort Union Trading Post National Historic Site

85   Gingras Trading Post State Historic Site

87   Hudson Townsite State Historic Site

89   Huff Indian Village State Historic Site

92   Icelandic State Park

95   International Peace Garden

98   Killdeer Mountain Battlefield State Historic Site

102   Knife River Indian Villages National Historic Site

105   Lake Jessie State Historic Site

106   Lake Johnson State Historic Site

108   Maple Creek Crossing State Historic Site

110   McPhail's Butte Overlook State Historic Site

111   Medicine Rock State Historic Site

113   Menoken Indian Village State Historic Site

115 Molander Indian Village State Historic Site
117 North Dakota Heritage Center
121 North Dakota Lewis and Clark Interpretive Center and Fort Mandan
125 Oak Lawn Church State Historic Site
126 Palmer's Spring State Historic Site
127 Pembina State Museum
130 Pulver Mounds State Historic Site
132 Ronald Reagan Minuteman Missile State Historic Site
136 St. Claude State Historic Site
137 Sitting Bull Burial
140 Standing Rock State Historic Site
142 Steamboat Warehouse State Historic Site
144 Stutsman County Courthouse State Historic Site
146 Sully's Heart River Corral State Historic Site
148 Sweden State Historic Site
149 Theodore Roosevelt National Park
154 Turtle Effigy State Historic Site
156 Turtle River State Park

159 Wadeson Cabin State Historic Site
160 Walhalla State Historic Site
162 Welk Homestead
164 Whitestone Hill State Historic Site
169 Writing Rock State Historic Site

171 Sibley and Sully's Northwest Indian Campaigns

181 **MAPS**
182 Northern Plains Tribes, 1850s–1860s
184 Trails Across Dakota, 1738–1903
186 Ethnic German Settlement, 1965
188 321st Strategic Missile Wing

189 Endnotes
190 More Places to Visit
202 Index by Theme
204 Guide Map to the Sites

Preface

THIS GUIDEBOOK is designed to help you find sites that will awaken your interest in North Dakota's lively and varied past. Unlike more populated states, North Dakota offers many unique opportunities to view locations where western history unfolded in the original context of rural landscapes. The "Introduction to North Dakota's Past," which follows on page 1, gives a brief overview of the state's history and explains how each listed historic site contributed to that history, from the time of the first human inhabitants through the late twentieth century, a span of 13,000 years. Because a number of the sites relate directly to the military activities of General Henry H. Sibley and General Alfred Sully and their troops during the 1863 to 1865 expeditions to Dakota Territory, a brief history of those military operations is provided on page 171.

This book primarily focuses on state historic sites and markers administered by the State Historical Society of North Dakota, as well as the two state museums. Also included are national, state, and tribal sites with historical significance and/or interpretive centers. Each historic site is marked by symbols indicating its significance in six areas of the state's history: Native Americans, Exploration and Settlement, Trade and Technology, State Government, Military Affairs, and Natural History. For each of these sites, the main entry contains a brief description and history of the site, with illustrations and maps show-ing the location, if accessible. All photographs not otherwise labeled are by Brian R. Austin.

Readers also will enjoy a trip to the North Dakota Heritage Center on the Capitol grounds in Bismarck, home to the State Historical Society of North Dakota. There, the three permanent galleries of the recently expanded State Museum tell the broad story of North Dakota's past through exhibits that highlight specific people, places, events, or artifacts that bring the state's history to life. For your research or questions about North Dakota history, you may wish to visit the State Archives and Historical Research Library in the Heritage Center as well. In the northeastern corner of the state, the Society's Pembina State Museum brings to light the agricultural history of the Red River Valley and the importance of the region in early trade networks, the lifeways of the Chippewa and Métis peoples, and the settlement of Euro-American immigrants.

Many of the state historic sites, a number of the state parks, the Lewis and Clark Interpretive Center, and federal parks and historical sites also house interpretive centers. These centers are noted in the site descriptions.

In the appendices to the book, there is a state map locating all the sites featured in the publication, along with several trail maps. There is also a listing of other historic sites, state and federal historical parks, and history museums to visit throughout the state. ◄

Foreword

WELCOME TO NORTH DAKOTA. We are happy that you are interested in exploring our great state and its wonderful history. This *Traveler's Companion* will give you information about state historic sites and points of interest that we hope you will enjoy. We are happy to share this information with you.

The diversity of attractions will amaze you. Discover Native American sites that illustrate 13,000 years of human habitation in North Dakota. You can visit village sites, like Double Ditch, where earthlodges provided homes for hundreds and sometime thousands of people, and trace the 800-year history of farming in North Dakota. Military sites in this book cross the state, from Fort Abercrombie in the east to Fort Buford near the western border. In the middle of the state is one of the best-preserved frontier forts in the country, Fort Totten, which later served as a school for Indian children. A new addition to our collection is Ronald Reagan Minuteman Missile State Historic Site near Cooperstown, which reveals the story of the Cold War. Other sites tell the story of the globe-spanning fur trade, early cattle ranching in North Dakota, and the development of new towns and settlements.

The Pembina State Museum is a beautiful site, located at the border between Canada, Minnesota and North Dakota. We are proud to have the Former Governor's Mansion restored and open to the public in the Capitol City of Bismarck. And, of course, there is the newly renovated and expanded North Dakota Heritage Center! This architecturally stunning building showcases North Dakota's world-class collections and presents the state's amazing heritage.

These are only a few of the many state historic sites in North Dakota administered by the State Historical Society. There are numerous state parks, city and county museums, national parks, and other historic sites, many also listed in this publication, to visit and appreciate. A great companion to this book is North Dakota Tourism's yearly *Travel Guide* that covers people, places, and events around North Dakota. We invite you to enjoy yourself as you visit these places and learn about who we are.

For more information regarding state historic sites please contact us at State Historical Society of North Dakota, 612 E. Boulevard Avenue 58505, call (701) 328-2666 or visit our web site at www.history.nd.gov.

For information about other interesting places to visit in North Dakota, you can also contact North Dakota Tourism at (800) 435-5663 or (701) 328-2525 or visit their website at www.ndtourism.com.

Have a great time in North Dakota,
MERLAN E. PAAVERUD, JR., *director*
State Historical Society of North Dakota ◄

Visiting the Sites

SOME OF THE SITES LISTED in this book are well developed, with interpreters, visitors' centers containing exhibits, furnished buildings, picnic areas, and other amenities. Others lie obscurely in pastures without a monument or fencepost to mark their existence. The descriptions of most sites in this book include maps and directions on how to visit them. The visitation information, including hours, presented in this book may change. Please check websites or contact the sites for updated information.

For a few sites such maps and descriptions are not provided. These places are currently closed to visitors because of lack of accessibility, concerns about preservation, or out of respect for Native Americans who hold some of these places sacred.

Many of the sites are small, consisting of less than an acre, and surrounded by privately owned property. We encourage you to view the locations of historic events from these sites. Exploration beyond these sites requires permission from the landowners.

We invite you to enjoy North Dakota's heritage but ask that you remember to take nothing but photographs. The past belongs to everyone, and all artifacts must be left behind for the information they represent and for future visitors to enjoy. It is illegal to search for or to remove artifacts from state, federal, or tribal property without a permit. ◄

Key to Using the Maps

Many of the maps include symbol legends. These are some of the more common maps elements you will see throughout the book. The letter/number codes in the white border of the North Dakota state highway map will make finding the directions to the sites easier.

Transportation
- Interstate highway
- Paved road or highway
- Gravel county road
- Dirt road

Physical Features
- *top* Terrace/cliff (closed points are top of the terrace)
- Lake/pond/slough
- River/creek/seasonal drainage

Urban Features
- Cities/towns
- Fence line
- Railroad

See Crowley Flint Quarry State Historic Site.

 Watch for this symbol for identification of **NATIVE AMERICAN** sites.

Introduction to North Dakota's Past

NORTH DAKOTA'S HISTORY began thousands of years ago when glaciers covered much of the northern hemisphere, including part of what is now North Dakota. The state's human heritage began with the first people who lived here. Most scientists believe the first inhabitants of North America entered the New World during glacial times, when Asia and North America were connected, by crossing a land bridge. Descendants of these first people, American Indians, have passed down oral histories that speak of their people originating in the New World.

The earliest artifacts found in this state were made by these first people, called Paleo-Indians, who hunted mammoth, very large bison, and other extinct large mammals. The Paleo-Indian period dates from 11,000 to 5500 B.C. At **Crowley Flint Quarry**, deep pits were dug by people seeking Knife River flint, a prized rock used for making stone tools.

As the Ice Age ended, the glaciers retreated to the north, and the climate became hotter and drier. Grasslands replaced the vast boreal forest. People adapted to the change in environment by hunting smaller game animals and gathering prairie plants during the Archaic period, dating from 5500 B.C. to 400 B.C. Artifacts that appear to date from this time period were discovered buried at the **Camp Hancock** site.

As the climate moderated and became similar to the modern environment, trade brought northern people into contact with other tribes living to the east along the Ohio and Illinois rivers. In addition to trade goods, new ideas traveled along these exchange routes. The concept of interring deceased relatives, together with exotic trade items, in artificial earthen hills called burial mounds, spread westward. From 400 B.C. until A.D. 1000, during the Woodland period, mounds were used to bury the dead. The **Pulver Mounds** and **Standing Rock** sites preserve Woodland period burial mounds.

The introduction of imported domesticated plants, such as maize, squash, pumpkins, sunflowers, and beans, transformed some of the nomadic Woodland people into village-dwelling people. During the Plains Village period (A.D. 1000 to 1780) the Nu'eta (Mandan), Hidatsa, Sáhniš (Arikara), and TsétsEhéstAhese (Cheyenne) lived in villages along the Missouri River and other major rivers. The early Mandan and Hidatsa villagers built rectangular houses near their river-bottom gardens between A.D. 1100 and 1500. **Menoken Indian Village, Huff Indian Village,** and **Fort Mandan Overlook** sites were occupied by these early farmers.

By the end of the sixteenth century, the rectangular earthlodge was replaced by a smaller, circular earthen house. **Double Ditch Indian Village, Molander Indian Village, Knife River Indian Villages,** and the village at the **Fort Clark** site are Mandan, Hidatsa, and Arikara earthlodge villages, occupied between A.D. 1490 and 1861.

Introduction to North Dakota's Past   >   1

Lapel pin with replica Lewis & Clark medal

Watch for this symbol for identification of EXPLORATION AND SETTLEMENT sites.

Although the dates of their creation are unknown, American Indian rock art sites are found at **Medicine Rock**, **Writing Rock**, and **Turtle Effigy** sites. These rare places preserve such important symbols as the outline of a turtle in boulders and numerous other animal figures carved into rocks.

In 1797 David Thompson mapped the Northwest Company's fur posts from the Souris River to the western shore of Lake Superior. The **David Thompson** site commemorates his visit to North Dakota. The Corps of Discovery, led by Captains Meriwether Lewis and William Clark, was the first governmental exploration of the Louisiana Purchase. This journey to the Pacific Ocean began in May 1804 and ended in September 1806. During the winter of 1804, the expedition stayed in an encampment called Fort Mandan, near the villages of the Mandan and Hidatsa Indians at the mouth of the Knife River. The **Fort Mandan Overlook** is near the site of their winter encampment. The **Missouri-Yellowstone Confluence Interpretive Center** at **Fort Buford** interprets the expedition's experiences in that area, as does the **North Dakota Lewis and Clark Interpretive Center and Fort Mandan**. Upon their return from the Pacific Ocean, they met just below the Confluence and visited the Mandan and Hidatsa villages in August 1806. Other early explorers, Joseph Nicollet and John C. Fremont, investigated the area between the Mississippi and Missouri rivers in 1839. The **Lake Jessie** site is one of their camps.

Explorers were quickly followed by fur traders. **Fort Clark** contains the remains of two early-nineteenth-century fur trade posts (Fort Clark Trading Post and Primeau's Post) that were established to trade with Mandan and, later, Arikara people at the village of *Mitu'tahakto's*. The **Fort Union Trading Post National Historic Site** was one of the most important trading posts along the river. **Gingras Trading Post** preserves the original 1840s home and trading post of Métis businessman and legislator Antoine Blanc Gingras. Norman Kittson's fur

Watch for this symbol for identification of NATURAL HISTORY sites.

Silky aster, a common wildflower.

trade warehouse from the 1840s at **Walhalla** is a preserved remnant of the commercial enterprise of the American Fur Company.

By the mid-nineteenth century, settlers were replacing the fur traders, and the military came to protect this Euro-American migration to the West. **Fort Abercrombie**, built in 1858, is the oldest military post in the state. In 1863 General Henry H. Sibley led an army across Dakota Territory, pursuing Sioux people who were believed to have participated in the US-Dakota War of 1862 (see **Sibley's and Sully's Northwest Indian Campaigns**). State historic sites from this expedition are **Buffalo Creek**, **Big Mound Battlefield**, **Lake Johnson**, **McPhail's Butte Overlook**, **Camp Arnold**, **Camp Atchison**, **Camp Buell**, **Camp Corning**, **Camp Grant**, **Camp Kimball**, **Camp Sheardown**, **Camp Weiser**, and **Camp Whitney**.

General Alfred Sully and the 2,000 soldiers in his command were also part of the military reprisal following the US-Dakota War. **Whitestone Hill** marks the site of the 1863 attack on Native Americans, the bloodiest engagement fought in North Dakota. **Fort Rice**, established in 1864, served as a base for Sully's 1864 and 1865 expeditions. As part of his 1864 expedition, Sully reluctantly escorted a wagon train bound for the Montana gold fields. **Sully's Heart River Corral** preserves rifle pits dug by frightened gold seekers left behind when the general attacked a Sioux encampment at **Killdeer Mountain**. Another wagon train of immigrants led by James L. Fisk, on its way from Fort Rice in 1864, was attacked by Hunkpapas who were angered by the attacks of Sibley and Sully. At a location now named **Fort Dilts**, the immigrants drew their wagons in a circle, built a sod wall around them, and waited to be rescued by the army.

Fort Ransom, established on the Sheyenne River in 1867, and **Fort Totten**, constructed near Devils Lake between 1867 and 1873, provided protection for settlers headed for western gold fields. At Fort Totten sixteen original structures still stand, and both the military mission of the post and its later use as an Indian boarding school are interpreted at the site. **Fort Stevenson State Park** was the site of a fort established on the Missouri River in 1867.

1880s infantry dress helment. SHSND 15905

Troops from **Camp Hancock** guarded workers building the Northern Pacific Railroad at Bismarck. Camp Hancock later became a supply distribution point for forts further out on the frontier. **Fort Abraham Lincoln State Park** marks the post from which Lt. Col. George Custer and the 7th Cavalry departed for the Little Bighorn in 1876. **Fort Buford**, the sentinel of the north from 1866 until 1895, was one of the forts protecting river transportation. The fort is also the place where the Hunkpapa Sioux leader Tȟatȟáŋka Íyotake (Sitting Bull) returned to the United States and entered military custody. The **Sitting Bull Burial** site near Fort Yates is a memorial to this Native leader.

Palmer's Spring, **Bismarck-Deadwood Stage Trail**, **Cannonball Stage Station**, **Steamboat Warehouse**, **Maple Creek Cross-**

Watch for this symbol for identification of MILITARY sites.

Introduction to North Dakota's Past ▶ 3

Cold War missile launch key

Watch for this symbol for identification of TRADE AND TECHNOLOGY sites.

ing, and **Brenner Crossing** mark sites associated with transportation, including historic overland travel, steamboats, and river crossings.

As the Indian Wars drew to a close, settlers began to move into the state in greater numbers. **Hudson Townsite, St. Claude, Sweden, Wadeson Cabin,** and **Icelandic State Park** commemorate late-nineteenth-century settlements and related activities. **Oak Lawn Church** marks the cemetery and foundation of an 1885 Presbyterian church. One of the oldest churches in Bismarck now stands at **Camp Hancock.**

The **Chateau de Morés, de Morés Memorial Park**, and **Chimney Park** commemorate the entrepreneurial efforts of a French nobleman who operated a cattle ranch and beef packing plant at Medora, Dakota Territory, in the 1880s. Nearby is **Theodore Roosevelt National Park,** named after the man who in 1884 purchased a ranch in the Badlands and later become the twenty-sixth president.

North Dakota's **Former Governors' Man-sion** was the first official residence for the state's governors. Built in 1884 and presently restored to its 1893 appearance, the home is open to visitors in Bismarck. Built one year earlier, in 1883, **Stutsman County Courthouse** is the oldest remaining courthouse in the state, located in Jamestown, North Dakota.

The **International Peace Garden** and **Turtle River State Park** are both sites of natural beauty that are enhanced with many structures and features constructed in the 1930s by CCC workers.

The newest state historic site, the **Ronald Reagan Minuteman Missile State Historic Site** near Cooperstown, served an important role as part of the United States' strategy of nuclear deterrence during the Cold War years.

In all, North Dakota's historic sites span nearly 12,000 years and tell a variety of stories about our history and heritage. The **Pembina State Museum** features exhibits on the fascinating history of the northeastern region of the state. The newly-expanded **North Dakota Heritage Center** in Bismarck covers the region's story through geologic time, early peoples, and into the modern era. We welcome you to visit our sites and experience the past. ◂

A goat was the symbol of the Nonpartisan League.

Watch for this symbol for identification of GOVERNMENT sites.

Introduction to North Dakota's Past

Historic Sites

- Native American Sites
- Exploration and Settlement Sites
- Natural History Sites
- Military Sites
- Trade and Technology Sites
- Government Sites

- Museum
- Restrooms
- Picnic
- Store

Big Mound Battlefield
STATE HISTORIC SITE

THE BIG MOUND BATTLEFIELD State Historic Site overlooks the site of the July 24, 1863, Battle of Big Mound. This was the first major battle fought in Dakota Territory by General Henry H. Sibley's Minnesota volunteers. It was the beginning of a week-long series of running battles that ended with the escape of the Native people to the west side of the Missouri River.(see **Sibley's and Sully's Northwest Indian Campaigns of 1863**). This historic site lies ten miles north and east of Tappen, Kidder County.

In July 1863 people of the Sioux Nation were heavily engaged in the seasonal buffalo hunts. Many Dakota people had joined their Yanktonai relatives on the rich hunting lands between the James and Missouri Rivers. Tȟatȟáŋka Nážiŋ (Standing Buffalo), Ožúpi (Sweet Corn), and other Sisseton and Wahpeton leaders who favored peace had led their people to the Big Mound area. Other groups of Dakotas, led by Iŋkpáduta (Scarlet Point) and other leaders who favored continued resistance, were also camped nearby to hunt. Some Hunkpapa Lakotas also crossed the Missouri River to join the hunt. They included Tȟatȟáŋka Íyotake (Sitting Bull), Phizí (Gall), and Nážin Maȟtó (Standing Bear).

Čhaŋhdéška Máza (Iron Hoop), a Sisseton Dakota, was one of the buffalo hunters at Big Mound. Years later he recalled, "One man on horseback went quite aways ahead and got up on top of a hill and immediately turned around and came back towards where we were, and said that all the Americans in the land were close onto us."[1] As Sibley's column approached the village on July 24, warriors and leaders from the village approached for a conference. Many of the Dakota people who had not been involved in the conflict in Minnesota wanted to discuss surrender. Others did not wish to do so, but a military clash did not appear eminent.

By noon, scouts had informed General Sibley that there were many Indians a few miles away. Sibley ordered the troops to set up camp (later named Camp Sibley) and to prepare trenches and breastworks (temporary fortifications) for defense.

Some of the scouts took up a position some four hundred yards south of the main camp,

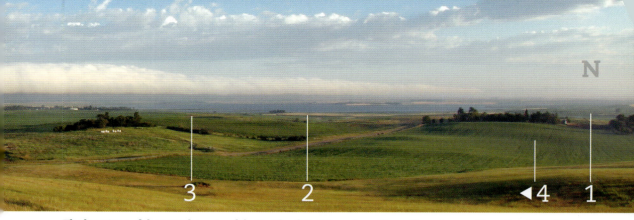

The locations of the initial events of the Battle of Big Mound are shown from due north on the right side of the photograph to south/southwest on the left. The battle continued toward the village, which was over the Coteau du Missouri (6) and to the left. From right, (1) Sibley's troops entered the area from the northeast. (2) The army was set to digging a fortification ditch south of modern-day Kunkel Lake. (3) This is the Big Mound State Historic Site marker, where Dr. Weiser was killed, ending the parley with the Sioux. The battle began here. (4) Sioux warriors advanced from the west and east (arrows) toward the fortifications. (5) McPhail's mounted Rangers passed over the edge of the Coteau to drive south and cut off the Sioux from escaping west into the lake area. (6) The Sioux retreated south along the top of the Coteau to their village and beyond. The image above shows less than a third of the battlefield.

where they were approached by Dakota Indians who asked to parley with General Sibley. Dr. Josiah S. Weiser, chief surgeon, 1st Regiment of the Minnesota Mounted Rangers, spoke Dakota and was assisting in the discussions when he was unexpectedly shot by one of the Dakotas. Both parties scurried for cover while exchanging gunfire and retreating to defensible positions. Several chiefs and elders, caught in the open, were killed by the soldiers. The chance of a peaceful outcome was gone.

The troops setting up camp formed into battle lines. Heavy fighting broke out in a large ravine running from the top of the surrounding plateau down to the campsite. Sibley moved up the hillside on the east side of the ravine

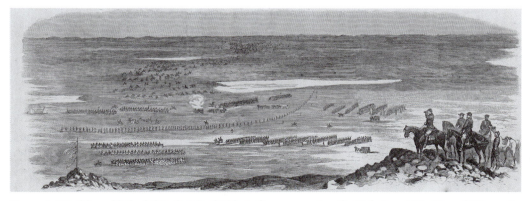

Harper's Weekly *published this sketch of Sibley's forces pursuing the Dakotas at Big Mound.* Harper's Weekly, *September 12, 1863*

Big Mound Battlefield

www.history.nd.gov

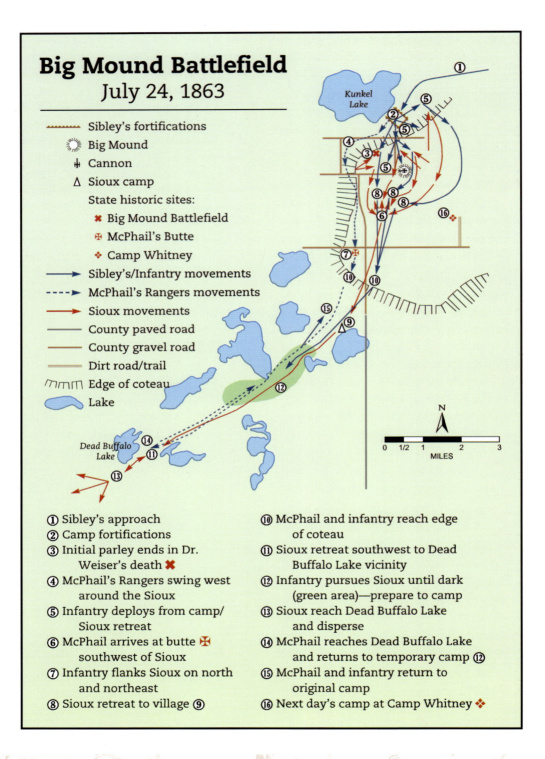

to establish a command post on high ground, accompanied by a battery of six-pound field cannons. From several progressively higher gun positions, the artillery shelled people concealed in the ravine, until the pressure of the artillery and advancing infantry forced them to retreat toward the top of the plateau.

On the eastern side of the battlefield, the Sixth Minnesota Infantry was advancing uphill against lighter opposition. When they topped the bluff line they turned south, driving the Sioux before them. On the west, McPhail's Rangers circled west out of Camp Sibley, cutting off attack from the exposed side of the camp. The cavalry established an effective blockade, preventing the Indians from slipping off the plateau to the west. The Seventh Infantry reached the top of the plateau and sandwiched the Sioux between themselves and McPhail on the west (see **McPhail's Butte Overlook**).

McPhail's troops pursued the Sioux to Dead Buffalo Lake, one mile north of the present-day town of Dawson. Receiving orders to return to the main camp, the troops marched most of the night to return to Camp Sibley. Sibley's men had fought their first major battle with no food and little water; some had covered nearly fifty miles during the engagement.

For their part, the Sioux warriors, by conducting a fighting retreat, had delayed the soldier's advance until their village could be evacuated. This successful retreat continued until they crossed the Missouri River. Included in the flight west was the Dakota family of Charles A. Eastman, who was four years old at the time. His later description of how the men fought to gain time for their families to cross the river is applicable to the whole journey:

The Washechu (white men) were coming in great numbers with their big guns, and while most of our men were fighting them to gain time, the women and the old men made and equipped the temporary boats, braced with ribs of willow. Some of these were towed by two or three women or men swimming in the water and some by ponies. It was not an easy matter to keep them right side up, with their helpless freight of little children and such goods as we possessed.[2]

The battlefield is now privately owned farmland with scant evidence of the conflict. The place where Dr. Weiser was killed is marked by a stone fence and granite headstone mounted on a boulder. ◄

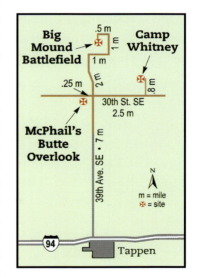

FROM TAPPEN, KIDDER COUNTY
North 9 miles on 39th Ave. SE, east 1 mile, north 1 mile, and west .5 mile. The site is marked by a red granite marker, in a cluster of bushes, 0.15 mile south on a dirt road.
GPS 47.022359, -99.628838

Bismarck-Deadwood Stage Trail
STATE HISTORIC SITE

FOR THREE YEARS, from 1877 to 1880, a thriving stagecoach and supply line ran between Bismarck, the western terminus of the Northern Pacific Railroad, and the Black Hills gold town of Deadwood in Dakota Territory. The Bismarck-Deadwood Stage Trail Historic Marker is found by a roadside stop on the north side of Highway 21, half a mile east of Flasher. The marker located at the stop explains the history of the trail and commemorates the brief economic boom associated with the trail.

After the Custer expedition discovered gold in the Black Hills in 1874, Bismarck merchants wanted a route for shipping goods and for transporting gold seekers to the hills. In late 1876, after a treaty opened the Black Hills to Euro-Americans, the Dakota Territorial legislature quickly authorized construction of a road from Bismarck to Deadwood. In 1877 the Northern Pacific Railroad Company and the Minnesota State Company formed the Northwest Express and Transportation Company to open a 240-mile trail to Deadwood.

The first stagecoaches left Bismarck on April 11, 1877, with sixty-eight passengers. Regular tri-weekly stages began May 2, 1877, and soon they were running daily. The company operated twenty-six Concord coaches and freight wagons pulled by 200 teams of horses. In addition to the freight and passenger revenue, the stage company was awarded an annual mail contract. The company erected an elaborate headquarters building in Bismarck at Main and Ninth Street and employed 175 men.

By the summer of 1878, the editor of a Denver newspaper proclaimed, "The Bismarck route from the Northern Pacific Railroad is the best patronized road running into the Black Hills." A year later all of the rooms in Bismarck hotels were filled with people bound for the Hills.

The transportation boom ended suddenly when the railroad reached Pierre, South Dakota. In 1880 the company moved most of its equipment to Pierre and opened an alternate line. After that the service on the Bismarck line was cut to tri-weekly trips and was soon abandoned.

All that remains to represent this flurry of activity are a few wagon ruts, such as those found near the Bismarck-Deadwood Stage Trail Historic Marker site, and the ruins of several stage stations (see **Cannonball Stage Station**). ◂

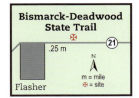

FROM FLASHER, MORTON COUNTY
East .25 mile on ND-21. The site is marked by an aluminum plaque on the north side of the highway.
GPS 46.458670,-101.219235

Stagecoaches carried passengers and freight from Bismarck to Deadwood. SHSND C0215

Brenner Crossing STATE HISTORIC SITE

BRENNER CROSSING State Historic Site lies near the military trail linking Fort Totten, near Devils Lake, to Fort Seward, near Jamestown. The actual river crossing, named for Ernest Brenner, below, is located several miles away on the Sheyenne River. The overlook is northeast of New Rockford, Eddy County, but is unmarked and has no visible remnants of the trail or other archaeological features.

Ernest William Brenner, born May 30, 1844, in Germany, came to the United States with his parents in 1848 and settled in Boston, Massachusetts. His varied career began as a page for two Massachusetts governors and later included scouting for Union General N. P. Banks during the Civil War. In 1868 he became the post trader at Fort Totten. He remained at the fort until 1882, when he left and began farming on the south bank of the Sheyenne River along the Fort Totten-Fort Seward trail.

SHSND C1396

In addition to farming, Brenner ran a river crossing and established a post office, where he served as postmaster. His enterprise was not a financial success, and in April 1887, he was appointed to be government agent (farmer-in-chief) at the Turtle Mountain Indian Reservation. The Brenner post office was discontinued April 23, 1887.

Brenner and his wife, Mary, had a daughter, Christina. Mary Brenner was the daughter of Pierre Bottineau, scout and guide, for whom the city and county are named. ◄

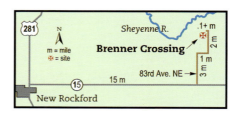

FROM NEW ROCKFORD, EDDY COUNTY

East 15 miles on ND-15, north 3 miles on 83rd Ave. NE, east 1 mile, north 2 miles, and west 0.1 mile. The site is unmarked on the south side of the road.

GPS 47.758945, -98.788934

Buffalo Creek STATE HISTORIC SITE

BUFFALO CREEK State Historic Site, in west-central Cass County, commemorates a point crossed by Sibley's expedition on August 15, 1863, on their way to Fort Abercrombie at the end of their summer campaign (see **Sibley's and Sully's Northwest Indian Campaigns**). This was not, however, the full expeditionary force that had entered Dakota Territory on July 2, 1863. Colonel Samuel McPhail and his 1st Minnesota Mounted Rangers were scouting down the James River and would return to Minnesota by a different route.

After leaving Camp Arnold, Sibley's men marched nine miles southeast in the growing heat of a mid-August day. The expedition crossed the Maple River and continued another three and one-half miles to Camp Stevens, where they stayed the night. The expedition was about to leave Dakota Territory after marching nearly one thousand miles, fighting three major battles and several skirmishes, and losing nine soldiers. Some have estimated the deaths among the Native American people they encountered during this expedition as approximately 300 people.

The modern Buffalo Creek State Historic Site is located about one-eighth mile east of the Maple River and about two miles northwest of the town of Buffalo. It is marked by a bronze plaque mounted on a boulder on the north edge of a gravel road. The plaque noting the expedition's crossing was installed in 1927 by the Dacotah Chapter of the Daughters of the American Revolution. ◀

FROM BUFFALO, CASS COUNTY
West 2.25 miles on 34th St. SE. The site is marked by a bronze plaque on a granite boulder north of the road.
GPS 46.919819, -97.604701

Camp Arnold STATE HISTORIC SITE

CAMP ARNOLD, located four miles north of Oriska, Barnes County, was the August 14, 1863, campsite used by the Sibley expedition during its return to Minnesota at the end of the summer campaign (see **Sibley's and Sully's Northwest Indian Campaigns**). It was named for Regimental Adjutant Captain John K. Arnold, 7th Minnesota Infantry.

Leaving their previous campsite early in the morning on August 14, the troops marched thirteen miles, following a trail left by one of Captain James Fisk's immigrant wagon trains. Although the day was cloudy and cool, it was also windy, and by noon the exhausted mules could go no further. The soldiers established a camp near the east end of Pickett Lake which, despite its poor water, supported a substantial population of muskrats.

Tired troops continued straggling into camp after a twelve-hour march. As they arrived, the men discovered that, as usual, there was no firewood and even the alternate fuel, "buffalo chips," was hard to find. However, the spirits of the troops were buoyed by the arrival of long-awaited mail and by the knowledge that they were finally on the way home.

Two soldiers, sixteen-year-old James Ponsford (Company D) and twenty-two-year-old Andrew Moore (Company B), 1st Regiment, Minnesota Mounted Rangers, died in camp on August 15. Ponsford died of disease and Moore of wounds received at the Battle of Big Mound on July 24, 1863. Although the site lacks a formal marker, headstones honoring these men are visible beside Highway 32. ◄

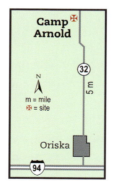

FROM ORISKA, BARNES COUNTY
North 5 miles on ND-32. The site is marked by a pink granite marker and two white marble headstones west of the road.
GPS 46.993362, -97.791066

Camp Atchison STATE HISTORIC SITE

CAMP ATCHISON, two and one-half miles south of Binford, Griggs County, served as a major base camp and landmark for the 1863 Sibley expedition. Prior to July 17 the principal thrust of the expedition had been toward Devils Lake, where alleged Indian participants of the US-Dakota War of 1862 were rumored to be living (see **Sibley's and Sully's Northwest Indian Campaigns**). On July 17, however, friendly Chippewa Indians visited General Sibley at Camp Pope and told him that the people he was pursuing had left the Devils Lake area and were fleeing for the Missouri River. Sibley decided that his army must move rapidly to catch them. To do so they needed to leave sick men, weak horses, the cattle, extra wagons, and other impediments behind.

On July 18 a nearly ideal base camp site was found on the northeastern shore of Lake Sibley. The site could be easily defended, had ample water, grass, and wood nearby, and was near known trails and landmarks, such as Lake Jessie and Devils Lake. The new camp was hurriedly established and was named for Captain Charles Atchison, the command's ordnance and assistant commissary officer. Fortified with substantial trenches and earthen breastworks, the camp was garrisoned by two companies from each of the three full infantry regiments, one company of cavalry, two cannons, plus the sick and disabled men, in all, a force of about 1,000 men.

The command suffered its first fatality that day when Private George E. Brent, a popular and respected veteran of Company D, 1st Regiment, Minnesota Mounted Rangers, was shot and killed by a second lieutenant from Company L of the same regiment. Some observers thought that the incident was accidental, but others thought it deliberate. The lieutenant was eventually arrested and held for court-martial.

On July 19 a courier from Fort Abercrombie brought mail for the troops. The spirits of the campaign were boosted with the announcement that Vicksburg, where some of these men had served only months before, had fallen to Union troops in a Mississippi campaign of the Civil War.

The following day, General Sibley and 1,450 infantry, 520 mounted rangers, 75 to 100 teamsters, pioneers and quartermaster's employees, six artillery crews, scouts, about fifty wagons, and 1,000 horses and mules marched off in pursuit of the enemy. While they were gone, Captain Burt led a reconnaissance to Devils Lake, where he unexpectedly captured the teenage son of Thaóyate Dúta (Little Crow), one of the Mdewakanton Dakota leaders of the previous year's conflict.

On August 10 General Sibley and his army returned to Camp Atchison. Stopping a few miles out, the men brushed and polished and broke out remaining uniform parts in order to make as impressive an entrance as possible for a command that had marched more than 300 miles on foot, and fought a series of battles and skirmishes in twenty-one days. For their part, the garrison and the expedition's drum corps welcomed the returning troops with flags and music. On the morning of August 12, the troops abandoned the camp and the graves of two of their comrades, Privates George E. Brent and Samuel Wanemaker.

Henry Frederic Jacob Knieff, a member of Sibley's expedition, drew this image of Sibley's base camp at Camp Atchison, July 18, 1863. MHS Collection I.360.1

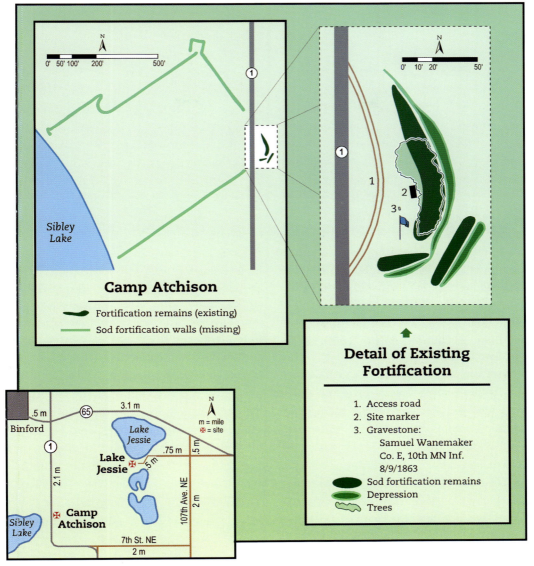

Camp Atchison State Historic Site bears little resemblance to the large field camp of 1863. A fieldstone monument and an aluminum marker identify the site. Only a small portion of the camp is preserved, including a small segment of the original rifle pits. The largest part of the site, with the graves of two soldiers, lies on private land across Highway 1 to the west. ◄

FROM BINFORD, GRIGGS COUNTY
East .5 mile on ND-65 to junction with ND-1, and south 2.1 miles. The site is marked by an aluminum plaque and white marble headstone east of the highway.
GPS 47.523986, -98.329294

Camp Buell STATE HISTORIC SITE

CAMP BUELL, the Sibley expedition's overnight campsite of July 3, 1863, was named for Major Salmon Buell, a battalion commander in the First Regiment, Minnesota Mounted Rangers (see **Sibley's and Sully's Northwest Indian Campaigns**). It is located north of Highway 13 at Milnor, Sargent County.

The diaries of two men provide details of troop life. By 4:30 A.M. on July 3, the military column had left Camp Parker and was marching toward Devils Lake through withering heat, engulfing dust, and unrelenting drought. Near the middle of the day's march, the troops discovered a pleasant lake with fresh, clean water. Two of the cavalry companies splashed their way into the lake, using sabers to catch fish.[3] By afternoon, the delights of "Fish Lake" were a distant memory when the mules began to give out and one company's pet dog died in the heat. After an eighteen-mile march, Camp Buell was established near a shallow, brackish lake, with water so "green and thick" that a quart of "vegetal matter" could be skimmed off of a kettle full of the muck.[4] The men had to dig wells on the beach, where sand clarified the seeping water for drinking.

As the troops arrived at Camp Buell, some men dropped out of formation and collapsed on the ground while others straggled in late into the night. The expedition's ambulances, which had been filled with exhausted men most of the day, traversed between the campsite and the route of march, picking up men too sick or weak to continue. The only consolation was that the expedition's sutler was allowed, this one night, to dispense whiskey, albeit at seventy-five cents a pint. Two years later the same site was used by the Third Illinois Cavalry, while en route from its temporary station at Fort Abercrombie to Devils Lake to participate in General Alfred Sully's 1865 expedition. ◄

FROM MILNOR, SARGENT COUNTY
West edge of Milnor, on ND-13. The site is marked by an aluminum plaque north of the highway.
GPS 46.248851, -97.45678

Camp Corning STATE HISTORIC SITE

CAMP CORNING was the July 16, 1863, campground of the Sibley expedition (see **Sibley's and Sully's Northwest Indian Campaigns**). The camp, named for the expedition's quartermaster, lies eight miles northeast of Dazey, Barnes County.

Before dawn that morning the troops left Camp Smith and discovered the trail left by Captain James L. Fisk's immigrant wagon train in 1862. Through the increasingly difficult terrain, the troops followed Fisk's trail, knowing that it would lead them to a good place to cross the Sheyenne River. As the troops descended from the plains into the wooded river valley, two companies of infantry were deployed as skirmishers to protect against attack. When the trail narrowed and progress slowed at the crossing, the train of wagons and soldiers formed a column nearly five miles long. As the troops waited to cross, a group of horsemen chased a small herd of elk toward the resting men. The soldiers captured one young elk and kept it as a mascot in one of the wagons.

After crossing the Sheyenne River, the expedition established Camp Corning near a small alkali lake. The brackish water was unfit for consumption. Shallow holes were dug near the lake shore to filter the water, but with only limited success. After three days without wood, the men began using "buffalo chips" as fuel for their cooking fires. When they learned that a trench full of the dried buffalo manure cooked as quickly as bituminous coal but without the sulphur or other disagreeable fumes, this became the major fuel source.

Currently, Camp Corning State Historic Site consists of a simple granite marker flanked by a stand of pines beside a county road ditch. ◄

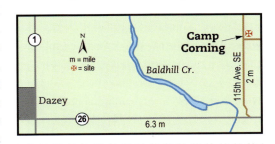

FROM DAZEY, BARNES COUNTY
East 6.3 miles on ND-26, and north 2 miles on 115th Ave. SE. The site is marked by a red granite marker under pines trees northeast of the intersection.
GPS 47.212018, -98.067613

Camp Grant
STATE HISTORIC SITE

CAMP GRANT, located six miles northwest of Woodworth, Stutsman County, commemorates the July 23, 1863, campsite used by the Sibley expedition (see **Sibley's and Sully's Northwest Indian Campaigns**).

After leaving about one-third of their forces behind at Camp Atchison, the column headed by General Sibley rapidly moved toward the Missouri River, where alleged participants of the US-Dakota War of 1862 were reportedly headed (see **Camp Atchison**). The army marched southwest, ascending the eastern slope of the Missouri Coteau, which was "very rough and rolling,"[5] comprising some of "the most broken and hilly country" yet crossed,[6] and arrived at the campsite about noon.

Within three hours, Camp Grant, named for Hiram Perry Grant, Captain of Company A, Sixth Minnesota Infantry, was established by "a small, muddy, stinking pond filled with rushes of tremendous size...."[7] The men were allowed to hunt wild geese and ducks, and they brought a large number of waterfowl into camp that night. A fresh water spring discovered in a ravine east of the camp furnished unusually clean water. Details were assigned to gather buffalo chips to burn as cooking fuel. Each detailed man "would take three or four ramrods" and search the prairie for chips, string them on the rods until each was full and deposit the collected strings at the camp's cooking area.[8]

During the evening, a disturbance beyond the outer picket line roused the camp. Some of the men gathering buffalo chips had lingered out beyond the guard lines until it was too dark to be assigned other camp duties. To end this malingering, the pickets (guards) were ordered to prevent any latecomers from entering the camp. The stragglers "set up a howling for the Corporal of the Guard," but they "were left to howl and without their supper until well after midnight," permanently ending that ploy during this campaign.[9]

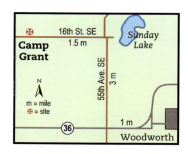

FROM WOODWORTH, STUTSMAN COUNTY
West 1 mile on ND-36, north 3 miles on 55th Ave. SE, and west 1.5 miles on 16th St. SE. The site is marked by a metal plaque on a boulder north of the road.
GPS 47.183022, -99.371746

Camp Hancock
STATE HISTORIC SITE

CAMP HANCOCK State Historic Site marks the location of a United States infantry post (1872–1877) and Quartermaster Depot/Signal Office (1877–1894), in present-day downtown Bismarck, at 101 East Main Avenue. The post was originally named Camp Greeley in 1872 in honor of Horace Greeley, editor of the *New York Tribune* and a liberal candidate for the presidency. The name, however, was short-lived. By October 7, 1873, the post was renamed Camp Hancock after the commander of the Department of Dakota.

The purpose of the post was to protect railroad supplies, equipment, and engineering crews of the Northern Pacific Railroad, as well as the citizens of Edwinton (renamed Bismarck in July of 1873). By 1883 the post had an added duty: to serve as a storage station for the quartermaster's supplies bound for posts up and down the river and for points further west.

A Signal Corps "reporting station" was established at Camp Hancock in 1874. The primary mission of the US Army Signal Corps was to transmit military messages. In addition, they maintained records of the nation's weather patterns. The last of the line troops were withdrawn from Camp Hancock on April 12, 1877. However, the post served the area's military needs by continuing to function as a quartermaster's depot and signal station, which required only a small staff of technical specialists.

After the post was decommissioned in 1894, the buildings were used as the head-

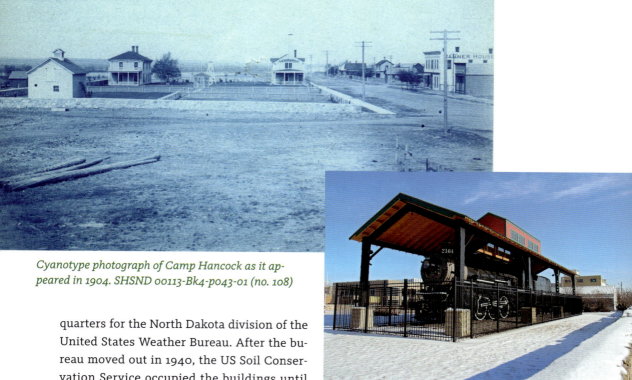

Cyanotype photograph of Camp Hancock as it appeared in 1904. SHSND 00113-Bk4-p043-01 (no. 108)

quarters for the North Dakota division of the United States Weather Bureau. After the bureau moved out in 1940, the US Soil Conservation Service occupied the buildings until 1949 when fire damage forced abandonment of the main building. In May 1951 the property was deeded to the State of North Dakota and opened as a state historic site by the State Historical Society.

In 1988 Society archeologists discovered evidence that the location was also a campsite for nomadic hunters and gatherers sometime during the Archaic period (5500 B.C.–400 B.C.). Although only a small area was excavated, it was evident that the inhabitants of the site worked locally available stones into chipped stone tools. Animal bone was smashed into small pieces and cooked for preparation of foods such as marrow (bone grease) and soup.

Today, the original Post Surgeon's quarters, which later became the Post Executive Officer's quarters, still stand on the site. This 1872 building is the oldest standing building in Bismarck. On the outside of the 1901 two-story Weather Bureau office building, which was built over the older building, is a "window" showing the original construction. Encircling the property is a stone fence constructed during the occupancy of the Weather Bureau. Camp Hancock site also exhibits a 1909 Northern Pacific locomotive (above), added in 1955, and St. George's Episcopal Church, which was moved to the site in 1965. The Church of the Bread of Life was built in 1881 and is the oldest standing church building in North Dakota. It has been restored to its original appearance.

Camp Hancock is listed on both the State Historic Sites Registry and on the National Register of Historic Places for its association with the military history of the state. The museum is free and open to the public May 16 through September 15. For more information or for specific hours, call (701) 328-9528.

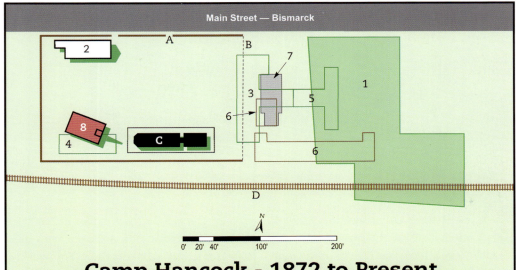

Camp Hancock - 1872 to Present

1. Camp site, August 1872.
2. Current museum; Officers' quarters, 1872-1877; Quartermaster's office and signal station, 1877-1894; Weather Bureau offices, 1894-1940.
3. Original barracks and mess rooms, 1872-ca. 1875.
4. Commanding Officer's quarters, 1872-1877; residence of Quartermaster's agent, 1877-1890s; residence of Weather Bureau station chief, 1890s-1920s.
5. Barracks addition, ca. 1875—kitchen, bakery, dispensary, hospital, laundry, and carpentry shop.
6. Warehouse (2), 1880s.
7. Weather Bureau station chief's residence, 1920s to 1950s.
8. Church of the Bread of Life, 1880 (moved to site, 1965).

A. Stone wall, ca. 1901 (Weather Bureau).
B. Chain link fence.
C. 1909 Northern Pacific Railroad locomotive (under shelter).
D. Railroad tracks (originally 1873 Northern Pacific track).

AT BISMARCK, BURLEIGH COUNTY
101 East Main Ave.
GPS 46.805167,-100.790275

Camp Kimball STATE HISTORIC SITE

CAMP KIMBALL, named for George C. Kimball, assistant quartermaster for the Sibley expedition, was the site of the expedition's encampment during the night of July 22, 1863 (see **Sibley's and Sully's Northwest Indian Campaigns**). The site is nine miles southwest of Carrington, Foster County.

Early in the morning on July 22, the army was on the trail. After leaving approximately 1,000 men and unnecessary supplies behind at Camp Atchison, the reduced force rapidly marched southwesterly toward the Missouri River, where the Indians they were pursuing were reportedly heading. The weather was cool and pleasant with just enough wind to blow away the dust raised by more than 2,000 men, 1,100 mules and horses, wagons, and artillery.

Along the way the column passed a site where Métis had slaughtered a herd of buffalo. A soldier's diary described the scene: "buffalo heads were lying around a few rods apart [for] as far as we could see."[10] Camp Kimball was established beside Pipestem Creek, which had clear, cool water that the men appreciated after subsisting on brackish lake water for many weeks.

That evening some of the expedition's scouts captured a Dakota man, one of their own couriers. A few days earlier he had been dispatched from Camp Atchison with messages for a nearby Dakota camp. For two days he had ridden toward the place where he had last seen the camp, but could not find it because the village had moved. This supported the rumors that the Dakotas had left the Devils Lake area for the Missouri River.

Today, Camp Kimball State Historic Site contains no marker, directional signs, or interpretation. The narrow plot of pasture bears little resemblance to a bustling military camp.

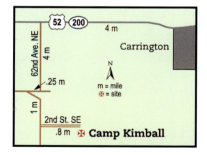

FROM CARRINGTON, FOSTER COUNTY
West 4 miles on ND-200/52, south 4 miles, west .25 mile, and southeast 1 mile on 62nd Ave. NE, and east .8 mile on 2nd St. SE, a dirt road. The site is unmarked on the south side of the road.
GPS 47.384131, -99.203811

Camp Sheardown
STATE HISTORIC SITE

A BRONZE MARKER identifies this site, named for Dr. Samuel B. Sheardown, regimental surgeon of the 10th Minnesota Infantry, as the July 14, 1863, campsite of the Sibley expedition (see **Sibley's and Sully's Northwest Indian Campaigns**). Located three and one-half miles southeast of Valley City, the marker sits on the southern edge of a county road ditch.

Reveille sounded at 2:00 A.M. on July 14, and troops began moving out of the previous night's camp, Camp Weiser, less than two hours later. In contrast to the intolerably hot days earlier, the weather was so cold that men riding horses and wagons wore overcoats all day long.

That day they marched eighteen miles toward Devils Lake, where Thaóyate Dúta's (Little Crow) band of Mdewakanton Dakotas was reportedly residing. One diarist noted that although they were still eighty to one hundred miles from Devils Lake, precautions were still necessary. After leaving Camp Hayes on July 12, the troops had been instructed to dig rifle pits and other fortifications each night. Nerves were becoming strained as evidenced by an incident in which a night sentry accidentally fired his rifle and set off "many ridiculous demonstrations."[11]

The day's march was considered very hard. One astute officer noted that they had passed over what was called "Bottineau's Mountain," not a rise which could be "measured by the eye" but, rather, the land rose in a "gradual ascent."

Approximately one and one-half miles east of the Sheyenne River, Camp Sheardown was established on high ground overlooking the lush river bottom, scenery thought to be "most beautiful." The soldiers' appreciation of the Sheyenne Valley was enhanced when the "Company C boys killed a fine doe elk, the meat of which was very fine."[12]

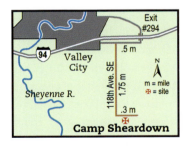

FROM VALLEY CITY, BARNES COUNTY
South 0.1 from I-94 exit #294 to frontage road, west .5 mile, south 1.75 miles on 118th Ave. SE, and east .3 mile. The site is marked by a bronze plaque south of the road.
GPS 46.891311, -97.970415

Camp Weiser STATE HISTORIC SITE

A SMALL granite marker identifies this site as the approximate location of the July 13 campsite of the Sibley expedition (see **Sibley's and Sully's Northwest Indian Campaigns**). It was named for Regimental Surgeon Dr. Josiah Weiser, 1st Minnesota Mounted Rangers, who was later killed at the Battle of Big Mound (see **Big Mound Battlefield**). Camp Weiser is located six miles southeast of Kathryn, Barnes County.

On July 13, 1863, the troops arose at 2:30 A.M. to leave Camp Wharton and march northwest toward Devils Lake. Unlike the scorching days that preceded, the weather was cool and cloudy. After marching twelve miles, the leading units began making camp at about 10:00 A.M. by a beautiful cluster of freshwater lakes. The lakes, larger than many they had seen in this country, provided good protection on three sides and held an abundance of frogs, a culinary treat for the men. There were also many ducks and geese, but an order prohibiting the discharge of firearms precluded hunting waterfowl.

Late in the afternoon, the cavalry arrived in camp with the weakened horses and mules that had been left behind at previous camps to recuperate from dehydration and heat exhaustion. By 9:00 P.M. a herd of some 140 cattle that had strayed thirty miles from camp were rounded up. Finally, the camp settled down for a few hours' respite before the next day's march.

Access is limited by road conditions, and there are no visitor services or interpretation at Camp Weiser State Historic Site.

FROM KATHRYN, BARNES COUNTY
East 3.2 miles on 51st St. SE, south 2 miles on 122nd Ave. SE, and east .8 mile on a dirt road. The site is marked by a pink granite marker inside a wood rail fence south of the road.
GPS 46.644691, -97.875285

Camp Whitney
STATE HISTORIC SITE

A stand of pines (arrow, left) indicates the position of Camp Whitney State Historic Site. A Grand Army of the Republic star (right) marks the site.

FOLLOWING THE Battle of Big Mound (see **Big Mound Battlefield and McPhail's Butte Overlook**), the Sibley expedition moved to Camp Whitney on July 25 (see **Sibley's and Sully's Northwest Indian Campaigns**). There they buried Dr. Josiah S. Weiser, whose death ignited the battle. His grave, marked by a cairn and headstone, and the historic site lie approximately ten miles northeast of Tappen, Kidder County.

The morning after the battle General Sibley watched tired men straggle into Camp Sibley and decided to wait until later in the day to move to a new camp. That morning Chaska, an Indian scout, and another scout returned with the body of Lieutenant Ambrose Freeman, who was killed the previous day while hunting with George Brackett, the expedition's beef contractor. Chaska, a witness to Freeman's death, helped Brackett hide in tall grass to avoid detection by the attacking Indians. The scout was instrumental in Brackett's escape.

Before the troops left at about noon, the bodies of Lieutenant Freeman, John Murphy, and Gustaf A. Stark were buried at Camp Sibley. Private Murphy had been killed by lightning during the battle, and Private Stark died from battle wounds. The troops marched four miles to a small, muddy, rush-filled lake where they found fresh grass, but no wood. The mood of the camp was sullen, with many of the men disappointed, if not openly angry, with General Sibley's decision to rest for the day while the Indians escaped.

A small isolated part of the original campsite is preserved. Possible remnants of rifle pits and defensive earthworks are visible. Access is limited by road conditions, and there are no visitor services or interpretation.

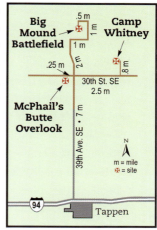

FROM TAPPEN, KIDDER COUNTY
North 7 miles on 39th Ave. SE, east 2.5 miles on 30th St. SE, and north .8 mile on a dirt road. The site is marked by a rock cairn, white marble headstone, and iron star, 0.14 mile west of the road.
GPS 46.993199,-99.589605

Cannonball Stage Station STATE HISTORIC SITE

THE CANNONBALL Stage Station was the fifth stop after Bismarck on the Bismarck-Deadwood Stage Trail. For a brief period from 1877 to 1880, a booming stagecoach line linked the westernmost stop of the Northern Pacific Railroad at Bismarck to the gold fields of the Black Hills. Built in 1877 by the Northwest Express and Transportation Company, the stage station overlooked the Cannonball River fifteen miles southeast of Carson, Grant County.

When the Northern Pacific Railroad ended its tracks at Bismarck in 1873, the town became the collecting point for travelers heading west or south. In 1877 one of the commercial transportation modes was a stagecoach line. The Bismarck-Deadwood stage quickly gained popularity because it ran directly to the gold fields of the Black Hills. By early summer 1877, daily stages were departing to the hills.

Whenever a stage arrived at the Cannonball Station, spent horses were replaced with fresh teams, and passengers stretched their weary bodies and ate the meager fare. Although this station was not as well equipped as the overnight stop at Cedar Creek, there was a barn and a log building. The station also served as a home to one employee.

Visitors stopping at the station today will find the remains of two dugouts (assumed to be the station building and an unknown building) and the rectangular outline of a barn. A quiet park on the east bank of the Cannonball River with a hand-pump water fountain and picnic table continue the tradition of hosting travelers at Cannonball Stage Station State Historic Site. ◅

FROM RALEIGH, GRANT COUNTY

South 4.75 miles on ND-31, west 2.7 miles on 77th St. SW, south 1 mile on 46th Ave. SW, west 4.75 miles on 78th St. SW, and south 4.6 miles on 53rd Ave. SW. The site is marked by an aluminum plaque, two dugouts, and a depression north of the road.

GPS 46.221664, -101.477583

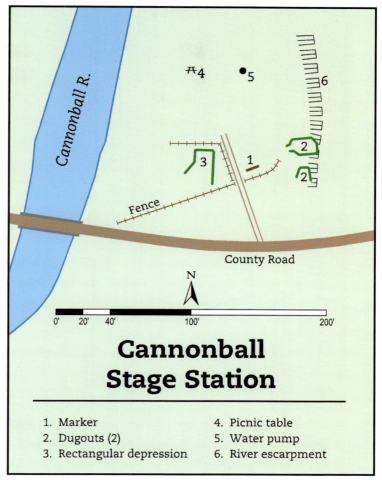

Cannonball Stage Station

1. Marker
2. Dugouts (2)
3. Rectangular depression
4. Picnic table
5. Water pump
6. River escarpment

The typical stage stop was a crude shelter with a sod roof, offering a welcome respite for travelers. SHSND A4193

Cross Ranch STATE PARK

LOCATED ALONG SOME of the last free-flowing and undeveloped stretches of the Missouri River, Cross Ranch State Park is rich in natural and cultural history, providing visitors an opportunity to learn about pre-history and history within the River Peoples Visitor Center at the park.

Cross Ranch State Park and the adjacent nature preserve contain the largest remaining tract of publically owned, undeveloped floodplain woodland on the Missouri River. Visitors discover a forest hundreds of years in the making, inhabited by a variety of animals, insects and plants. The park and nature preserve also comprise an archaeological district designation on the National Register of Historic Places.

The Mandan and Hidatsa Indians developed rich cultures, but were devastated by diseases that came with the white man. Significant archaeological sites within the park and preserve include earthlodge villages, winter villages, bison kill sites and processing stations, campsites, and burial mounds. In October of 1804, the Lewis and Clark Expedition camped across the river from the park. Just a few miles upstream, northwest of present-day Washburn, the expedition made its winter camp at Fort Mandan.

In 1879 A. D. Gaines, a professor of classical literature and a land agent for the Northern Pacific Railroad, purchased over 11,000 acres in the area. The community of Sanger, originally named Bentley, was established at this time, providing rail and steamboat services—all that remains today of the once-thriving town are a handful of abandoned buildings.

Bob and Gladys Levis acquired ownership of the Gaines Ranch in 1956, renaming it the Cross Ranch. The Nature Conservancy subsequently purchased that property in 1984. The Nature Conservancy and Burlington Northern Railroad donated land to create the boundaries of present-day Cross Ranch State Park. North Dakota Parks and Recreation Department manages the nearly 600-acre park, while the Conservancy oversees about 6,000 acres as a dedicated state nature preserve.

The River Peoples Visitors Center features displays about the natural and cultural history of the park and also supports administrative offices. The building is shaped like President Theodore Roosevelt's famous Maltese cross brand, which was acquired by Bob Levis and currently owned and registered by the Nature Conservancy.

The park and nature preserve are connected by an extensive hiking trail. Throughout the year log cabins and yurts are available for rent, along with primitive camp sites for RVs and tents. During peak camping season, water hydrants are available along with showers, flush toilets, and a sewage dump station. A limited number of electrical campsites are available at the Sanger Campground, located south of the main park. This campground is designed for boaters and anglers wishing to explore the Missouri River.

Cross Ranch State Parks hosts special events such as the Missouri River Bluegrass and Ol' Time Music Festival. More than fifteen miles of hiking trails allow extensive exploration of the park, river and nature preserve. Mountain bikes, motorized vehicles and horses are precluded on park and preserve trails. Cross country skiing, on the park's ten miles of groomed trails, is a popular winter pastime.

Campground reservations can be made on the North Dakota Parks and Recreation Department website at www.parkrec.nd.gov or by calling (800) 827-4723. For more information about Cross Ranch State Park check the website or call the park at (701) 794-3731.

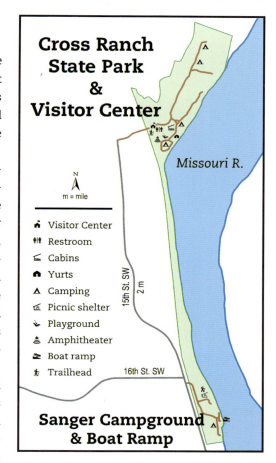

FROM HENSLER, OLIVER COUNTY
South 5.6 miles on 28th Ave. SW, east 4.5 miles on 16th St. SW, and north 2 miles on 15th St. SW to the Cross Ranch access road, east of the road.
GPS 47.213656, -100.999603

Crowley Flint Quarry STATE HISTORIC SITE

FOR 11,000 YEARS American Indians dug into gravel deposits in western North Dakota seeking Knife River flint, a coffee-colored, translucent stone. Knife River flint was easily made into tools for hunting game, preparing food, and many other purposes. Several of these ancient quarry pits are preserved at Crowley Flint Quarry State Historic Site along Spring Creek, located near Golden Valley, Mercer County.

Knife River flint is one of the most important lithic (stone) materials used by prehistoric people in North America. Its attractive color, ability to hold a sharp edge, and easy procurement made it popular. Although the only major source of this stone is in North Dakota along Spring Creek, artifacts made from Knife River flint have been found in archaeological sites as far away as Pennsylvania. The flint reached these distant locations through trade. American Indians exchanged flint for other exotic goods, such as marine shells from the Gulf of Mexico, copper from the Great Lakes, or obsidian from the Yellowstone Park area.

At Crowley Flint Quarry, rounded holes mark the locations where Knife River flint was removed by prehistoric stone quarriers. Numerous depressions, measuring nine feet across and up to three feet deep, testify to the industry of these early peoples. The first Ice Age inhabitants of the state dug shallow pits in the loose glacial gravel and removed cobbles of the prized stone. Later, American Indians had to dig deeper to find suitable flint cobbles, because much of the best material had already been removed. Early in the first century A.D., digging Knife River flint was a well-organized activity. It was the predominant lithic material in the area until it was replaced by metal tools introduced by European traders.

Although Crowley Flint Quarry has not been excavated by archeologists, archaeological excavations of similar sites have produced a wealth of information about North Dakota's first widely traded natural resource. Because Crowley Flint Quarry is surrounded by private land and lacks an access road, it is currently closed to the public. ◄

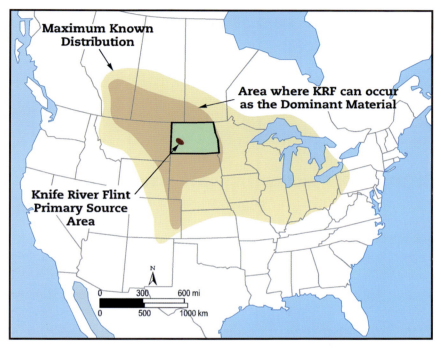

Map showing the location of the Knife River flint (KRF) primary source area and the distribution of KRF artifacts in archaeological sites in North America.

Artist's rendition (detail) of flint quarrying.

David Thompson STATE HISTORIC SITE

DAVID THOMPSON, explorer, fur trader, and the first European to explore the entire length of the Columbia River, was called by a contemporary "the greatest geographer of his day in British America." To honor his accomplishments as a geographer and astronomer, the David Thompson State Historic Site is marked by a granite globe atop a rectangular granite base, northeast of Velva, McHenry County.

David Thompson was born in Westminster, England, on April 30, 1770. He was educated at London's Grey Coat School, a charitable institution. When he was fourteen years old, he left school and became an apprentice to the Hudson's Bay Company to learn clerking, surveying, and hunting. In 1797, after finishing his apprenticeship, he joined the Northwest Company, a formidable fur trade competitor of his former employer.

As part of his first trading assignment, an attempt to establish a trading alliance with the Mandan and Hidatsa Indians living in a group of villages at the mouth of the Knife River (currently **Knife River Indian Villages National Historic Site**), Thompson was entrusted with the task of mapping the Northwest Company's posts and determining their relationship to the American border. Although the border was understood to run westward along the 49th parallel to the Rocky Mountains, it was still in dispute. Thompson passed near the historic site while on this assignment, leaving the Souris River a short distance west of the confluence of the Wintering River with the Souris on December 23, 1797. Thompson's surveys and observations from this expedition led to the first reliable map of the region from the west bend of the Souris River to the western shore of Lake Superior, a map used by Lewis and Clark during their expedition across North America.

Thompson continued his explorations and observations for another fifteen years, and

www.history.nd.gov   34   David Thompson

the exploration of the Columbia River was his most famous accomplishment. In 1812 Thompson retired from active trading and exploration. He settled in Terrebonne, Quebec, where he finished his great map of the Northwest. For ten years Thompson worked for the International Boundary Commission and during his last years, he completed the narrative of his experiences. He and his Scots-Cree wife, Charlotte, raised thirteen children. David Thompson died February 10, 1857.

The David Thompson State Historic Site is enclosed by a barbed wire fence and overlooks the beautiful Souris River Valley. The Great Northern Railroad donated the land to the state and commissioned and erected the monument, which was dedicated on July 17, 1925. The pedestal under the globe bears the following inscription:

> 1770 DAVID THOMPSON 1857
> Geographer and Astronomer
>
> Passed near here in 1797 and 1798 on a scientific and trading expedition. He made the first map of the country which is now North Dakota and achieved many noteworthy discoveries in the Northwest.

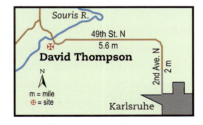

FROM KARLSRUHE, McHENRY COUNTY

North 2 miles on 2nd Ave. N and west 5.6 miles on 49th St. N. The site is marked by a granite globe south of the road.

GPS 48.122380, -100.750101

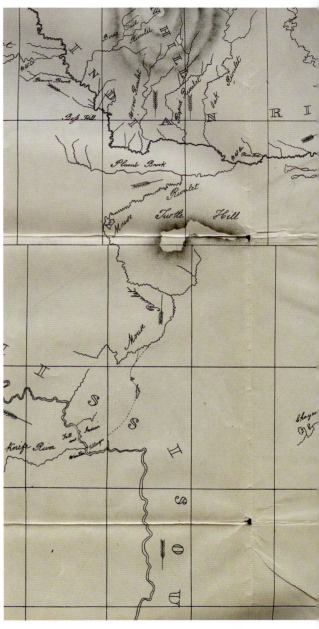

A detail from a map drawn by David Thompson for the North West Company. Taken from David Thompson's Narrative of His Explorations in Western America, 1784–1812, *J. B. Tyrrell, editor (Toronto: The Champlain Society, 1916). ID SHSND 971.2 T37t, Map 1*

De Morés STATE HISTORIC SITE

THE 128-ACRE de Morés State Historic Site interprets the capitalistic enterprises of Antoine de Vallombrosa, the Marquis de Morés, a proud and visionary French nobleman. The site is comprised of three separate parts: the Chateau de Morés and the interpretive center (⅛ mile west and ⅛ mile south of Medora), Chimney Park (west edge of Medora), and de Morés Memorial Park (downtown Medora).

The Marquis arrived in Dakota Territory on April 1, 1883, with exciting ambitions. The European aristocrat embarked on several innovative projects in the rugged badlands. Like other venture capitalists who were investing money in western cattle ranching, he was intent on increasing his fortune. Among his business enterprises were ranching, a meat-packing plant with refrigerated cars for shipping beef, a salmon-brokering enterprise, a stagecoach line, and a freighting company. He also founded a new town, which he called Medora in honor of his wife.

The Chateau de Morés is a twenty-six-room, two-story, frame building which served as a rustic summer home for the de Morés family from 1883 to 1886. This large ranch house rests amidst a landscape of enchanting beauty. Overlooking the Marquis's town and enterprises, the house was ready for his wife's arrival in the spring of 1884. During their short stays in Medora, elegant aristocratic furnishings, such as oriental carpets and fine china, accommodated the family and their wealthy visitors, including Theodore Roosevelt. For three summers the family lived there, traveling to New York or overseas during the winters. Among their pastimes were hunting, music, and art, common diversions of nineteenth-century aristocrats.

By 1886 the Marquis's business ventures ended, and, as a result, the family visited Medora only a few more times. Caretakers maintained the house in the owners' absence, and, for a period in the 1920s, the Vallombrosa family allowed the chateau to be used as a tourist boarding house. In 1936 the family donated the Medora properties to the state, with the State Historical Society of North Dakota designated as trustee. The Civilian Conservation Corps and Works Progress Administration (WPA) participated in the restoration of the chateau between 1936 and 1940, and it opened to the public as a historic site in 1941. The Chateau de Morés is presently a historic house museum containing original furnishings and personal effects of the de Morés family. The site has been listed on the National Register of Historic Places since 1975.

In Medora the State Historical Society also main-

Medora, the Marquise de Morés. SHSND 0042-60

The Marquis de Morés. SHSND 0042-089

tains Chimney Park, the ruins of the Marquis's meatpacking plant. Situated on the west edge of Medora, the packing plant was part of the Marquis's most ambitious and inventive project: to supply high-quality meat to the nation's consumers quickly and economically by processing it locally and shipping it to market in refrigerated railroad boxcars. The site once contained a corral, the meatpacking plant, a slaughterhouse, three icehouses, several outbuildings, and a railroad spur. Although the plant could process 150 beef carcasses per day, finding cattle that were fit to butcher was difficult due to the ongoing drought in the badlands. The plant closed in November 1886, a failure due to fierce competition from major Chicago-based packers, the effects of bad weather and drought, and the Marquis's inattentiveness to his business interests. When the Marquis left Medora in 1886, his plant was abandoned. The building burned in 1907. A tall, native-brick chimney still stands in silent tribute to this early attempt to capitalize on the meatpacking business.

De Morés Memorial Park in downtown Medora displays a bronze statue of the Marquis de Morés, erected in 1926. In the late 1930s, WPA efforts to improve the property included a stone wall with hand-hammered ornamental iron pickets and entrance gate that encircles the park, flagstone walkways, and landscaping with native vegetation.

De Morés State Historic Site is open to the public daily from May 16 through September 15, and Tuesday through Saturday from September 16 through May 15. The interpretive center near the Chateau de Morés features two museum galleries, an eight-minute introductory video, and a museum store. North Dakota Heritage Foundation members and children age five and under are admitted free; school groups pay reduced admission.

For more information, contact the site supervisor, De Morés State Historic Site, Box 106, Medora, North Dakota, 58645, or call (701) 623-4355.

AT MEDORA, BILLINGS COUNTY

The Chateau de Morés access road is east 1.25 miles from I-94 exit #24, south of US-10. The interpretive center is .3 mile south and the Chateau is a further .6 mile.

Approaching Medora from the east I-94 exit #27, or from the west exit #24, on US-10, the de Morés Packing Plant site access road is .5 mile east of the Little Missouri River, on the north side of the highway.

The de Morés Memorial Park is located in the southeast corner of the intersection of Main Street and 3rd Ave. in Medora.
GPS 46.912450, -103.534738

The interpretive center features exhibits on regional transportation and de Morés's experiments with refrigerated cars for shipping beef.

www.history.nd.gov   38   ◂   De Morés

De Morés Packing Plant 1886

1. West icehouse
2. Ice elevator
3. Kill rooms
4. Coolers
5. Chill rooms
6. Salt room
7. East icehoouses (2)
8. Fertilizer room
9. Cooper shop
10. Fertilizer press & small slaughterhouse
11. Office
12. Open space
13. Vats
14. Well
15. Boiler & engine room
16. Vats

Oblique view of plant

The diagram shows the layout of the meatpacking plant in 1886. Meatpacking operations began in October 1883. De Morés enlarged the plant in 1884, and when the new facility was completed in September 1885, it was said to be the most modern and complete for its size in the country. All that remains of the plant are the foundation ruins and the tall native brick chimney, preserved as part of the de Morés State Historic Site.

Pictured on the opposite page is the bronze statue of the Marquis de Morés, erected in the de Morés Memorial Park in June 1926, a gift of the Marquis's sons, Louis and Paul Vallombrosa.

De Morés > 39   www.history.nd.gov

Double Ditch Indian Village
STATE HISTORIC SITE

DOUBLE DITCH INDIAN VILLAGE State Historic Site, overlooking the Missouri River from its east bank, seven and one-half miles north of Bismarck, was once a large earthlodge village inhabited by Mandan Indians from the late 1400s to 1785. Double Ditch is one of the most spectacular archaeological sites in the Northern Plains. The remains of earthlodge and refuse mounds up to ten feet high, are enclosed by concentric fortification ditches (dry moats) and log palisades.

A massive smallpox epidemic swept the interior of North America about 1781–1782. This catastrophe was apparently responsible for the abandonment of Double Ditch and all the other Mandan villages near the Heart River. The Mandans moved to new villages farther upriver near the Knife River.

The Mandans are one of the famous agricultural tribes of the Missouri Valley region. According to Mandan oral history, their people lived in seven to nine villages near the mouth of the Heart River prior to Euro-American contact. The Mandan population in this area probably totaled 10,000 or more during this time. The Mandans developed a rich and elaborate culture based on gardening and bison hunting. They raised corn, beans, squash, pumpkins, sunflowers, and tobacco on the river bottoms below their villages.

These villages were centers of trade among themselves, nomadic Indian neighbors, and Euro-American traders. Items traded in prehistoric times include garden produce, hides, and meat. Other non-perishable trade items include stone raw materials such as Knife River flint, obsidian, and catlinite (pipestone); shells from the Pacific, Gulf, and Atlantic coasts; and native copper from the upper Great Lakes region. The earliest known direct contact between white traders and Mandan

Indians occurred in December of 1738 near present-day Bismarck.

The Mandans built dome-shaped houses of logs and earth which, when collapsed, appear as circular depressions. Earthlodges typically were thirty-five to forty-five feet in diameter, though they varied from twenty to sixty-five feet, and housed a family of eight to twenty people. The men usually decided how large an earthlodge would be, and the women did most of the building. To build an earthlodge, a wooden framework was erected, and then covered with layers of willow branches, grass, and finally, earth. It took about one hundred and fifty trees to build one earthlodge.

The compact, fortified settlements attest to the fierce warfare between villagers and surrounding nomadic tribes that is reported in early historic records. Four fortification systems have been identified at Double Ditch.

They consist of a deep moat and a wall of wooden posts that formed a palisade. Natural features, such as steep terrain and river banks, also were used for added protection. The outermost ditch represents the earliest occupation at the site, and encompassed approximately twenty-two acres. There were probably one hundred and sixty homes and perhaps 2,000 residents within the outer fortification system. The innermost ditch protected the last settlement at Double Ditch, and only encompassed four acres, or about one-fifth its original area. Only thirty-two clear earthlodge depressions are present inside this ditch, indicating a population of less than four hundred persons.

A Harvard University research group conducted archaeological investigations at the site in 1905. They excavated several middens (garbage heaps), a complex of storage pits, portions of lodge floors, and parts of the outer

Detail of artist's rendition of the village at Double Ditch as it may have appeared in A.D. 1550. SHSND mural by Robert Evans.

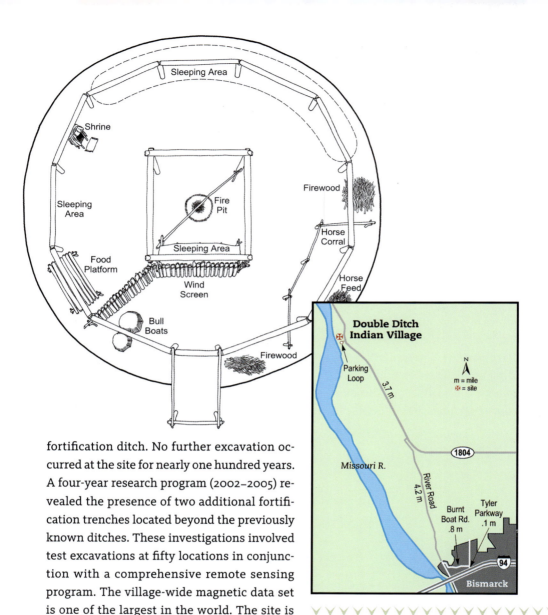

fortification ditch. No further excavation occurred at the site for nearly one hundred years. A four-year research program (2002–2005) revealed the presence of two additional fortification trenches located beyond the previously known ditches. These investigations involved test excavations at fifty locations in conjunction with a comprehensive remote sensing program. The village-wide magnetic data set is one of the largest in the world. The site is now known to have been substantially larger, was occupied longer, and is far more complex than previously thought. It was acquired by the State Historical Society of North Dakota in 1936 and is listed in the National Register of Historic Places. Interpretive signs at the site provide a walking tour along the village perimeter. ◂

FROM I-94 EXIT 157 AT BISMARCK, BURLEIGH COUNTY

North 0.1 mile on Tyler Parkway, west .8 mile on Burnt Boat Road, north 4.2 miles on River Road, jogging to the east, and north 3.7 miles on ND-1804. The site access road and parking loop is 0.1 mile west of the highway.

GPS 46.934631, -100.898695

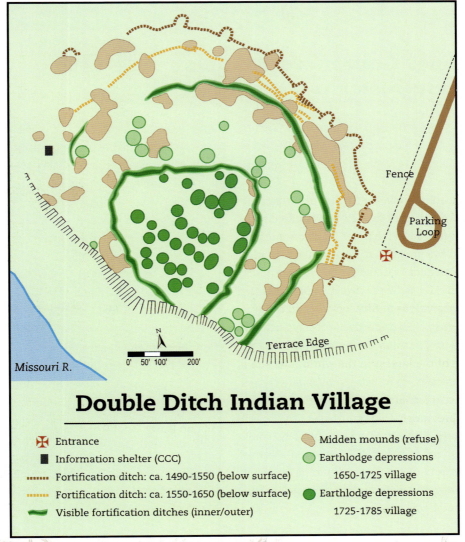

Double Ditch Indian Village

✠	Entrance	Midden mounds (refuse)	
■	Information shelter (CCC)	Earthlodge depressions	
┈┈	Fortification ditch: ca. 1490-1550 (below surface)	1650-1725 village	
┈┈	Fortification ditch: ca. 1550-1650 (below surface)	Earthlodge depressions	
━━	Visible fortification ditches (inner/outer)	1725-1785 village	

Former Governors' Mansion
STATE HISTORIC SITE

THE FORMER Governors' Mansion State Historic Site, located at 320 Avenue B in one of Bismarck's earliest residential areas, commemorates the North Dakota governors who resided there from 1893 to 1960. Constructed in 1884 by Bismarck businessman Asa O. Fisher, the mansion was purchased by the State of North Dakota in 1893 for the sum of $5,000. The third governor of the state, Eli C. D. Shortridge, and his family moved in later that year.

Twenty chief executives subsequently occupied the mansion, with each family bringing their own changes in its decoration and, in some cases, its structure. The mansion was the site of social gatherings and state functions, and was the official home of the governor during a time in which the city of Bismarck changed dramatically. The mansion was one of the first houses in the city to have indoor plumbing, electricity, and steam heat. The carriage house from "horse-and-buggy" days was converted into a garage in the 1920s. As the mansion became more and more antiquated, funds for construction of a new residence were finally approved by the 1955 Legislature. The last governor to occupy the mansion was John E. Davis, who moved to a new ranch-style governor's residence on the capitol grounds in 1960.

After its abandonment as the chief executive's home, the mansion was used as the first outpatient health clinic in the state. In 1963 the clinic was part of a national pilot program for community mental health centers, initiated by President John F. Kennedy. State Health Department records were housed in the home until 1975, when the building was transferred to the State Historical Society. Restoration work returned the building's exterior to its 1893 stick-style Victorian appearance. It is now an architectural and historic landmark in Bismarck and is listed on the National Register of Historic Places.

Restoration of the building's interior focuses on preservation and the evolution of interior decor in this historic house. This unique approach has allowed original furniture and objects from different administrations to be placed together within the building, reflecting the mansion's continuous history. Interior walls, ceilings, and floors have exposed areas showing the many layers of paint and wallpaper used in the house over the years. Intensive research and documentation has helped to provide an understanding of the way the house was decorated during various periods.

The Former Governors' Mansion is open May 16 through September 15 and the second Friday and Saturday of each month in the winter, or by appointment with the site supervisor. Video programs of the mansion's history and restoration are featured. Admission is free, and donations are accepted. Partial funding for the mansion's restoration and maintenance is provided by the Society for Preservation of the Former Governors' Mansion. For more information and specific hours, contact the site supervisor at (701) 328-9528. ◄

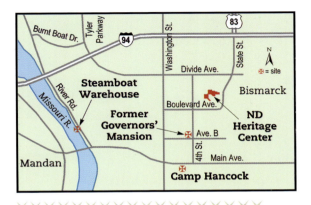

AT BISMARCK, BURLEIGH COUNTY
320 East Ave. B
GPS 46.810844, -100.786465

The carriage house, which later became a garage, houses exhibits on the move from horse and buggy to automobile.

Former Governors' Mansion ➤ 45   www.history.nd.gov

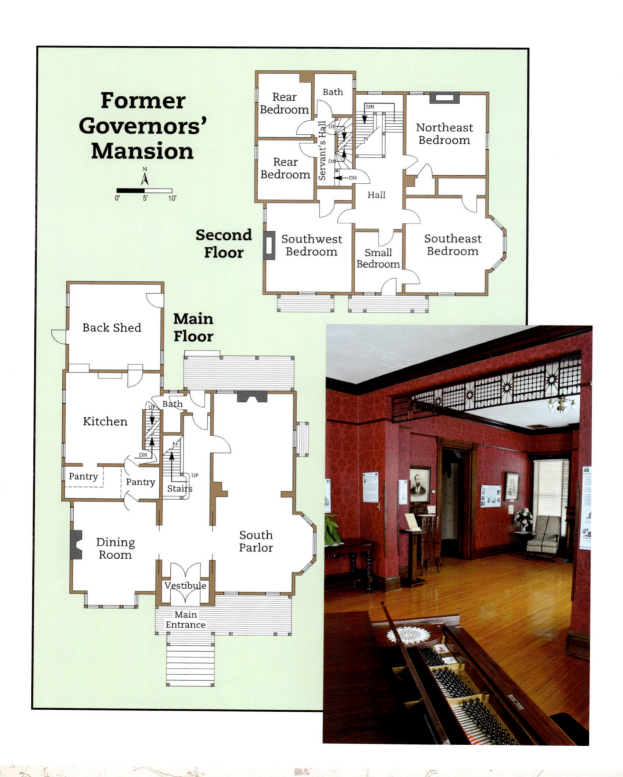

Fort Abercrombie
STATE HISTORIC SITE

FORT ABERCROMBIE was established on August 28, 1858, on the Red River in Dakota Territory by Lieutenant John J. Abercrombie. Because of the threat of flooding in the bottomland area originally chosen for the fort, it was reestablished in 1860 at its present location on a high west bank of the Red River in what is now Richland County. It is located approximately one-fourth mile east of the town of Abercrombie on Richland County Road #4. After the post was abandoned in 1877, the town of Abercrombie formed one-half mile west of the historic fort location.

Known historically as "the Gateway to the Dakotas," Fort Abercrombie was the first permanent United States military fort established in what was to become North Dakota. It was also the only post in the area to be besieged by Dakota (Sioux) warriors during the US-Dakota War of 1862 (see **Sibley's and Sully's Northwest Indian Campaigns**). During the conflict, Minnesota Volunteer soldiers manned the fort when area settlers sought shelter there. The "regular" US Army soldiers had been withdrawn during the Civil War and had been replaced by the Minnesota Volunteer Infantry. The fort was not protected by blockhouses or a palisade during the siege, but these defensive structures were constructed soon afterward.

The fort guarded the oxcart trails of the fur trade era, military supply wagon trains, stagecoach routes, and steamboat traffic on the Red River (See map on pages 184–85). It also was a supply base for gold-seeking expeditions across Dakota into Montana. Fort Abercrombie served as a hub for several major transportation routes through the Northern Plains.

After the fort was abandoned in 1877, fort buildings were sold and removed from the site. The state purchased the site in 1903. A Works Progress Administration (WPA) project in 1939–1940 reconstructed three blockhouses and the stockade and returned the original military guardhouse to the site. Major portions of the WPA project have been refurbished and the site reinterpreted.

From the interpretive center on the north side of the county highway, visitors may access a walking path around the interior square of the parade ground to view the reconstructed palisade, two reconstructed blockhouses, the original guardhouse, a reconstructed cannon bastion, several "ghosted" buildings, and informational markers describing the site.

Fort Abercrombie State Historic Site is open free of charge year-round. The interpretive center is open daily during the summer season from May 16 through September 15. An admission fee is charged for the interpretive center. State Historical Society of North Dakota Foundation members and children five and under are admitted free; school groups pay reduced admission.

For more information during the summer season, contact the site supervisor, Fort Abercrombie State Historic Site, P.O. Box 148, Abercrombie, North Dakota 58001, or call (701) 553-8513. Information may also be obtained throughout the year by contacting the State Historical Society of North Dakota at (701) 328-2666 or going to the Society's web site. ◀

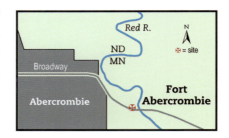

FROM ABERCROMBIE, RICHLAND COUNTY

East on Broadway to southeast edge of Abercrombie. The site interpretive center is north of the road.
GPS 46.444770, -96.718665

Exhibits interpret life in a frontier military post.

In 1870 Father J. B. M. Genin, Catholic Missionary Apostolic to the Native people of the region, arranged a gathering of Dakota and Chippewa leaders at Fort Abercrombie. They negotiated a treaty of peace after a breakout of hostilities in north-central Minnesota. SHSND 978.4 N814, V2, Part 2, p34a

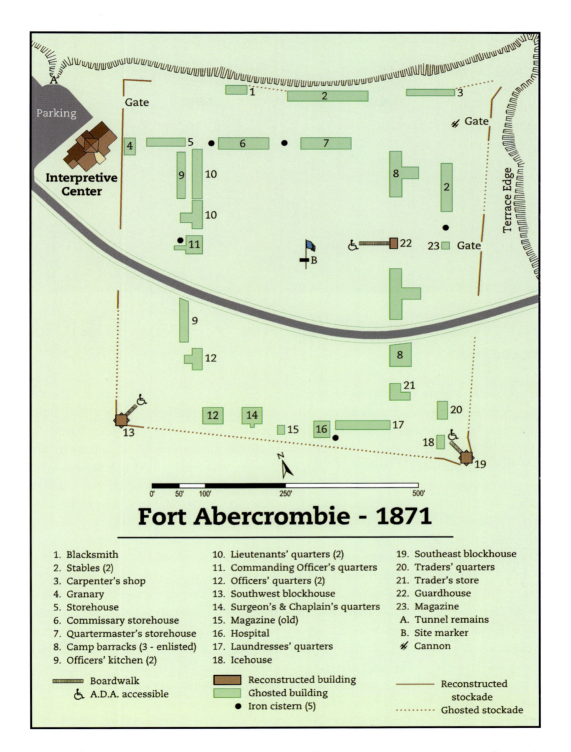

Fort Abraham Lincoln
STATE PARK

RICH IN BOTH military and American Indian history, Fort Abraham Lincoln State Park is located seven miles south of Mandan on Highway 1806. It is perhaps best known as the home of Lt. Colonel George Armstrong Custer's Seventh Cavalry, but long before the military post was built, this location was home to the Mandan Indian people who lived at On-A-Slant Village.

On-A-Slant Village is one of several traditional settlements in which the Mandan lived for many generations near the mouth of the Heart River, so named for its central place in the Mandan world. Recent studies indicate that On-A-Slant Village was settled in the 1500s and was occupied continuously for at least two hundred years. Lewis and Clark camped across the Missouri River from this village and recorded in 1804 that the settlement was in ruins, having been abandoned about twenty-five years earlier. They built Fort Mandan upriver near *Mitu'tahakto's*, where they befriended Chief Sheheke (White Coyote), who was born at On-A-Slant in 1766. Sheheke traveled with Lewis and Clark to Washington, D.C. in 1806, returning to the Mandan Villages in 1809. Lodge depressions are visible at On-A-Slant, along with six reconstructed earthlodges, including a very large circular earthlodge that is intended to convey the size of a community ceremonial lodge. Guided tours of the lodges are available, including interpretive exhibits on hunting, gardening, and children's activities. Exhibits about the life of the Mandans and the activities of the military fort are housed nearby in a stone museum constructed in the 1930s by the Civilian Conservation Corps (CCC). The

CCC also built a number of other facilities at Fort Abraham Lincoln including blockhouses, shelters, lodges and roads.

Fort McKeen, an infantry post, was built in 1872 on the bluffs overlooking the Missouri River and the former Mandan village. In 1873 a cavalry post was constructed on the flats along the Missouri and the combined installations were renamed Fort Abraham Lincoln. That same year, Lt. Colonel George Armstrong Custer arrived as the commander of the new post. With room for six companies of men in three barracks, seven officers' quarters, stables, granaries, commissaries, and quarters for Arikara Indian scouts and the fort's laundresses, the post housed about 1,000 people.

With Fort Abraham Lincoln as a base, Custer led surveying expeditions, in violation of the Fort Laramie Treaty of 1868, into the Yellowstone country and the Black Hills, sacred country of the Dakota and Cheyenne. The 1874 Black Hills Expedition confirmed the presence of gold in the Black Hills, setting in motion a flood of illegal immigration to the Black Hills. When President Grant and his military advisers determined that 1876 would be the year to force all the free bands of Indians onto reservations, Custer's Seventh Cavalry marched to Montana Territory. On June 25, 1876, Custer and his men were defeated at the Little Bighorn. Custer and his closest friends and relatives at Fort Abraham Lincoln were among the 265 US soldiers killed.

The home in which George and Libbie Custer lived at the fort has been reconstructed and is open for tours. From the front porch, visitors can watch the activities on Cavalry Square. Visitors can also inspect the reconstructed commissary store, granary, enlisted men's barracks, stables, and the infantry blockhouses overlooking the Missouri Valley.

A modern campground is located in a wooded area adjacent to the Heart River with picnic sites and playground equipment as well as two cabins. About 9.5 miles of trails include Scouts Trail, honoring American Indians serving in the US cavalry and infantry, and a paved bike and walking trail has connections to Mandan and Bismarck. Seasonal living history demonstrations, interpretive programs, and guided tours of the Custer home are features of the park, and the reconstructed Commissary Storehouse includes concessions, a bookstore, and a coffee shop. Other activities include shoreline fishing and horseback riding, as well as a nearby off-highway vehicle trail leading to historic Fort Rice. Interpretive tour hours are 9 A.M. to 7 P.M. Memorial Day through Labor Day, 9 A.M. to 5 P.M. in September, 1 to 5 P.M.

Officers and wives on the steps of the commanding officer's quarters, 1875. SHSND A1936

OPPOSITE: *Fort Lincoln in the distance and On-A-Slant Indian Village at lower left, from the southeast corner of the Fort McKeen terrace.*

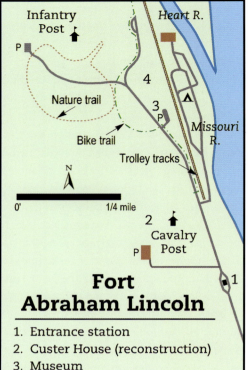

in October, and by appointment the rest of the year. There is a daily entrance fee and annual park permits are available. Additional fees are charged for Custer House tours, for campsites, and for some living history demonstrations. For more information about Fort Abraham Lincoln State Park, contact the North Dakota Parks and Recreation Department, 1600 East Century Avenue, Bismarck, North Dakota 58503, call (701) 328-5357, or visit http://www.parkrec.nd.gov.

Fort Abraham Lincoln

1. Entrance station
2. Custer House (reconstruction)
3. Museum
4. On-A-Slant Indian Village
P Parking
▲ Camping area

FROM MANDAN, MORTON COUNTY

From the intersection of Main St. and ND-1806, south 6.9 miles, past the ND Veterans Cemetery, and north .5 mile on Fort Lincoln Road to the park entrance.
GPS 46.75909, -100.84548

The reconstructed Fort McKeen blockhouse

Fort Buford and the Missouri-Yellowstone Confluence Interpretive Center

FORT BUFORD, located near present-day Williston, was one of a number of military posts established to protect overland and river routes used by immigrants settling the West. It served as the sentinel on the Northern Plains for twenty-nine years.

On June 15, 1866, soldiers under the command of Brevet Lieutenant Colonel William G. Rankin commenced building a new fort in Dakota Territory. It was named after the late Major General John Buford, hero of Gettysburg. By the end of November, the finished fort consisted of a 360-foot-square stockade enclosing log and adobe buildings, which was constructed to house a single company garrison.

Although historically the Fort Buford region was claimed by the Hidatsas, the Lakotas controlled the area after the Hidatsa population was decimated by smallpox. The Lakotas, angered by the establishment of the fort, attacked a work party at the sawmill on December 21, 1866. Raids continued sporadically throughout the winter. Post Surgeon James P. Kimball noted that these attacks were led by Sitting Bull.

Construction of a larger fort to house additional troops began in 1867. The old stockade was partially demolished and original buildings were either remodeled or torn down. The new buildings were constructed from handmade adobe bricks and green lumber, which caused deterioration within three years. The deplorable condition of the buildings, as well as increased Indian attacks, necessitated the construction of an expanded fort in 1871–1872. As part of the third construction phase, the post was designed to be a ten-company post but was ultimately built to house six companies.

While the fort construction was underway, the Northern Pacific Railroad resumed survey activities west of the Missouri River. The Yellowstone expeditions of 1871–1873 and the Black Hills expedition of 1874 violated the Treaty of 1868. The Sioux were provoked and felt the president of the United States "must stop the railroad," because it would destroy or chase away wildlife. They would not let the invasion of their lands go unchallenged.

By late 1875, the situation had deteriorated to the point that the secretary of interior asked the secretary of war to force Indians onto their respective reservations. This action began the Sioux Wars of 1876–1879 that included the defeat of Custer at the Battle of the Little Bighorn and Tȟatȟáŋka Íyotake's (Sitting Bull) flight into Canada. Sitting Bull struggled to maintain his independence, but lack of game for hunting and the desire of his people to return to their relatives led him to return to Dakota Territory. Thirty-five families, 187 people in all, traveled with Sitting Bull to Fort Buford, where on July 19, 1881, the great chief surrendered his Winchester .44 caliber carbine to Major D. H. Brotherton, Fort Buford's commander.

The role of the army at Fort Buford for the next fifteen years was to protect survey and construction crews of the Great Northern Railway, to prevent Indians and Métis from crossing the international boundary from Canada, and to police the area against outlaws.

African Americans served in the frontier Army from Civil War times and were an essential part of frontier posts. Called "buffalo soldiers" by Native Americans, they soon adopted the name as a term of pride. Two regiments of buffalo soldiers were stationed at Fort Buford. The 25th Infantry arrived at the post in 1891, and were joined by the 10th Cavalry in 1892. Both regiments were posted at Fort Buford until it was decommissioned. The important role of the buffalo soldier in the fort's history is increasingly recognized.

By 1895 the buildings were so dilapidated that repairs would be too expensive. The fort was no longer necessary for the army's mission, and was abandoned on October 1, 1895.

Three original buildings stand at Fort Buford State Historic Site: the stone powder magazine, wood-frame officers' quarters, and a wood-frame officer-of-the-guard building. Inside the officers' quarters is a museum exhibit featuring artifacts and displays about the frontier military and Fort Buford's role in the history of Dakota Territory. Although the original guardhouse is gone, its "ghost" remains. A metal framework outlines the building, showing its original size and shape. A reconstructed enlisted men's barracks recreates the feeling of the living quarters as they existed in 1878. Guided tours of the barracks are offered

West row of officers' quarters, Fort Buford, 1880. SHSND D0189-2

Rotunda of Missouri-Yellowstone Confluence Interpretive Center

throughout the summer season. To the west of the site is a Masonic interpretive center that tells the history of the Masons at Fort Buford.

Southwest of the museum is the fort cemetery. After the fort was abandoned, all military personnel buried at Fort Buford were disinterred and removed to the national cemetery at the Little Bighorn Battlefield National Monument in Montana. Reconstructed wooden headboards mark the graves where soldiers were once interred. As far as it is known, the graves marked by civilian headstones still contain the bodies of those interred there. Nearby is a picnic area and campground.

The Missouri-Yellowstone Confluence Interpretive Center just east of the fort itself features two exhibit galleries, interpretive programs and activities, a museum store, and a plaza overlooking the pristine confluence of the Missouri and Yellowstone rivers. Permanent exhibits explore the geography and geology of the area, prehistoric life, and the Lewis and Clark journey, the fur trade era, Fort Buford, and the development of the modern-day irrigation and energy industries. A large rotunda contains murals featuring quotes from the Lewis and Clark journals and paintings of the Missouri River landscape by Colonel Philippe Régis de Trobriand, commanding officer of Fort Stevenson in the late 1860s. A temporary exhibit gallery highlights the diverse collections of the State Historical Society.

Fort Buford and the Missouri-Yellowstone Confluence Interpretive Center are located just off Highway 1804 about twenty-five miles southwest of Williston, Williams County. The fort is open to the public, free of charge, throughout the year; there is an admission fee for the Interpretive Center and to tour the fort buildings. North Dakota Heritage Foundation members and children five and under are admitted free; school groups pay reduced admission. For more information, contact the site supervisor, Fort Buford State Historic Site and the Missouri-Yellowstone Confluence Interpretive Center, 15349 39th Lane NW, Williston, North Dakota, 58801, or call (701) 572-9034.

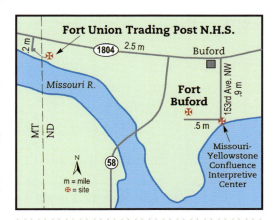

FROM BUFORD, WILLIAMS COUNTY
South .9 mile on 153rd Ave. NW. The interpretive center is southeast of the road. For Fort Buford, travel west .5 mile from the interpretive center. The fort site is north of the road.
GPS 47.986457, -104.000251

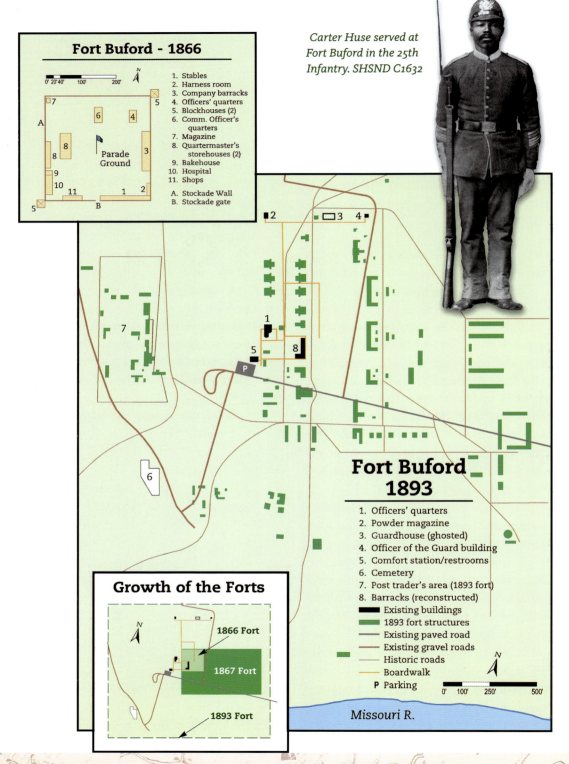

Fort Clark Trading Post
STATE HISTORIC SITE

FORT CLARK TRADING POST State Historic Site is one of the most important archaeological sites in the state because of its well-preserved record of the fur trade and American Indian life in the first half of the nineteenth century. The associated historical record is virtually unparalleled in the wealth of information about the place and its inhabitants. The archaeological remains of the earthlodge village, cemetery, and fur trade posts (Fort Clark and Primeau's Post) are protected at the site, located one and one-quarter mile west of the town of Fort Clark.

The story of the site begins in the summer of 1822 when the Mandans built a village of earth-covered homes on a high terrace along the west bank of the Missouri River at the confluence of Chardon Creek and Clark's Creek. They called their new community *Mitu'tahakto's* (pronounced me-toot-a-hank-tosh), meaning first village or east village. The village overlooked gardens tended by the village women who grew crops of corn, beans, squash, pumpkins, and sunflowers. Tobacco was the only crop grown by men, who were primarily responsible for hunting bison and other game. After the fall harvest, the villagers moved to a winter village sheltered in the wooded Missouri river bottom. Each spring, they returned to *Mitu'tahakto's* to plant their crops. Today, the Missouri River channel has meandered one mile to the north of the site.

In 1830–31, James Kipp, an employee of the American Fur Company, built Fort Clark south of the Mandan village to trade with the Mandans, Hidatsas, and Arikaras. Crows, Cheyennes, and Yanktonais also frequented the post during its thirty-year operation. The 1833 rectangular fort measured 110 feet by 100 feet and was protected by a palisade and blockhouses. Inside the fort were a bourgeois house, where the head trader Francis A. Chardon lived, and other fur trade buildings. Between 1834 and 1839, Chardon kept a journal of his life at Fort Clark, which records the tragic history of the site, including the

In 1905 a Mandan man, I-ki-ha-wa-he (Sitting Rabbit), created a map of the Mandan villages that had existed along the Missouri River, including this image of Mitu'tahakto's. The village leader, Ke-ka-nu-mak-shi (Crow Chief), is depicted above the village. Fort Clark is barely visible on the left edge. SHSND 800. Sitting Rabbit also created the map of Missouri River villages, shown above and below. SHSND 679

1837–1838 smallpox epidemic. Archaeologists have documented two later expansions before 1848.

The first steamboat to journey to the Upper Missouri, the *Yellow Stone*, arrived at Fort Clark in 1832 and delivered 1,500 gallons of liquor and other trade goods. Among the passengers on its maiden voyage was the artist George Catlin, who would witness the Okipa ceremony of the Mandans. Catlin's portraits of Mahto Topé (Four Bears), Mint, and Mah-Tó-He-Hah (Old Bear) are among his most

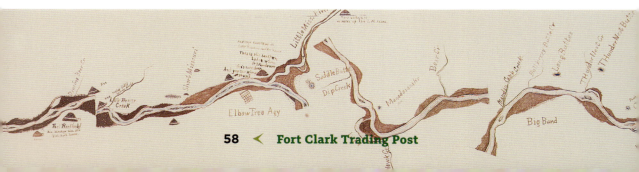

distinguished artworks. The *Yellow Stone* returned to St. Louis carrying 100 packs of beaver pelts and bison robes from the fort. A year later German scientist and explorer Prince Alexander Philipp Maximilian of Weid-Neuweid, accompanied by artist Karl Bodmer, also visited Fort Clark. Maximilian's journals and Bodmer's exquisite watercolors each document the vitality of the place and its peoples. Bodmer's paintings capture the essence of the location.

Steamboat traffic was important in transporting goods and visitors, but it also brought disease. On June 19, 1837, the steamboat *St. Peters* docked at Fort Clark carrying passengers infected with smallpox. The disease swept through the Mandan village, killing about 90 percent of the inhabitants. In mid-August, at the height of the smallpox epidemic, the survivors fled to join the Hidatsas near the mouth of the Knife River, abandoning the village at Fort Clark.

Although also devastated by the 1837 epidemic, approximately 50 percent of the Mandans' neighbors, the Arikaras, survived. In the early spring of 1838 they moved into the abandoned Mandan village to trade at Fort Clark and grow their crops. Tragically, an outbreak of cholera in 1851 and another of smallpox in 1856 further reduced their population. The Arikaras used the village as their summer home until they founded Star Village near Like-A-Fishhook Village and Fort Berthold in 1862.

Meanwhile, a smaller fur trade post, Primeau's Post, had been constructed on the south side of the Arikara village in 1850 by a competitor, Harvey, Primeau, and Company of St. Louis. The fort was located between Fort Clark and the Arikara village. Charles Primeau, a former employee of the American Fur Company, started the competing company. Artists Carl Wimar and William Hays sketched Fort Clark and Primeau's Posts in 1859 and 1860, near the close of their operation.

After the south half of Fort Clark burned in 1860, the owners purchased Primeau's Post, which they operated until 1861. Later that year, Primeau's Post and the Arikara village were abandoned after an attack by the Dakotas. Passing steamboats scavenged firewood from the abandoned fort until at least 1865. Formative anthropologist Lewis Henry Mor-

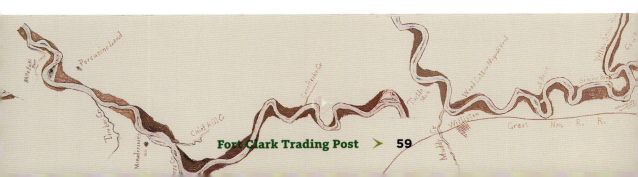

Aerial view of Fort Clark and Mitu'tahakto's as they exist today.

gan visited the site after its abandonment in June 1862.

Today Fort Clark is listed on the National Register of Historic Places. More than 2,200 surface features represent the ruins of houses, graves, storage pits, and other cultural remains. The location of houses in *Mitu'tahakto's* is indicated by a series of large, shallow, doughnut-shaped depressions. There are approximately 100 depressions marking the locations of Mandan and Arikara lodges. In the center of the village near the terrace edge is a flat, central plaza used by the Mandans for ceremonies. Later, the Arikaras built a large, ceremonial lodge in the plaza. It is clearly visible as the largest earthlodge depression. Small depressions within the village mark subsurface storage pits, called cache pits, which were used for storing garden produce. Surrounding the village is a shallow fortification ditch which, combined with a palisade, protected the village from attack. Unlike palisades protecting prehistoric villages, the stockade at *Mitu'tahakto's* was outside the ditch.

Beyond the fortification ditch are large, irregular pits from which soil was dug to cover earthlodges. Also visible are several small lodge depressions. Native visitors, who often came to trade, camped outside the village. The long, low ridges shown on the map are difficult to see on the ground but are believed to outline horse corrals.

At the southeastern edge of the village are the remains of Primeau's Post. Between the post and the remains of Fort Clark is a large earthlodge depression, the location of the home of Pierre Garreau. Garreau, the Arikara stepson of a French-Canadian trader, raised vegetables inside a picket fence beside his home to sell to Fort Clark personnel. The fence abuts the palisade that protected Fort Clark from attack.

Clusters of small, circular depressions and doughnut-shaped mounds near the railroad tracks mark graves. This unmarked cemetery, with approximately 800 graves, testifies to the tragedy of epidemics that nearly annihilated the occupants of the Mandan and Arikara villages.

Modern restrooms, a picnic area, and an observation deck are located at the site. Interpretive signs provide additional information. For more information, contact the State Historical Society of North Dakota at (701) 328-2666.

FROM FORT CLARK, OLIVER COUNTY
West 1.25 miles on ND-200A and north 1 mile on access road. The site is east of the road.
GPS 47.252997, -101.278528

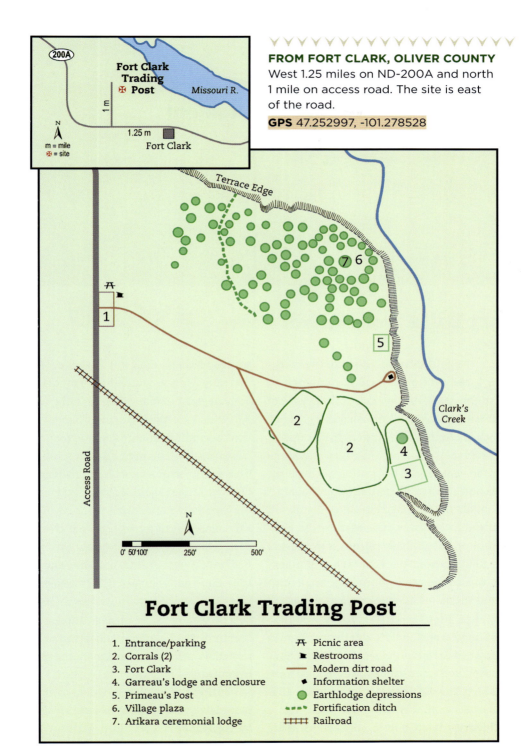

Fort Clark Trading Post

1. Entrance/parking
2. Corrals (2)
3. Fort Clark
4. Garreau's lodge and enclosure
5. Primeau's Post
6. Village plaza
7. Arikara ceremonial lodge

- Picnic area
- Restrooms
- Modern dirt road
- Information shelter
- Earthlodge depressions
- Fortification ditch
- Railroad

Fort Dilts STATE HISTORIC SITE

FORT DILTS State Historic Site marks the site of a dramatic episode in North Dakota history where gold seekers in an embattled wagon train circled their wagons and waited for rescue by the cavalry. Fort Dilts appears today much as it did more than one hundred years ago in its pristine setting eight miles northwest of Rhame, Bowman County.

On July 15, 1864, Captain James L. Fisk, US Quartermaster Corps, led ninety-seven wagons out of Fort Ridgely, Minnesota, for the gold fields of western Montana and Idaho. This was a dangerous journey of more than a thousand miles during an era of increased hostilities after the US-Dakota War of 1862 (see **Sibley's and Sully's Northwest Indian Campaigns**). Fisk proposed to follow a new, shorter route across unmapped territory from Fort Rice, Dakota Territory, west to the Bighorn River, in what is now Montana.

Believing that General Sully and his army preceded them, Fisk left Fort Rice, Dakota Territory, with a small military escort of fifty convalescent soldiers. Eighty miles west of Fort Rice, Fisk discovered that General Sully's trail veered north, and he realized that the train was now reliant upon their small escort. The wagon train was attacked by Hunkpapa Lakotas on September 2, nearly 180 miles from the fort. Sully's attack on the Indian village at Killdeer Mountain had occurred five weeks earlier, and the running battle through the Badlands between Sully and the Lakotas had lasted into early August. The Lakota warriors were in no mood to allow any military-escorted wagon train to pass through their territory. The Lakota attack left nine people from the wagon train dead and three seriously wounded.

During the following two days, the train moved twelve miles while constantly harassed by the Hunkpapa warriors. Maȟtó Watȟápa

(John Grass), a Lakota leader, was present at the siege.

One member of the wagon train was wounded. Progress was slow, and soldiers had to use a howitzer to clear the way in front of the train. On September 4, the members of the wagon train found a defensive point where they could dig in until reinforcements could arrive from Fort Rice. During the next few days, the men cut sod and stacked it to a height of six and one-half feet in a defensive perimeter 300 feet in diameter. It was christened Fort Dilts by members of the wagon train in honor of Corporal Jefferson Dilts, who died from his wounds and was buried in the entrenchments. Two other soldiers, Marma D. Betts and Thomas C. Williamson, were also buried in the sod wall.

Lieutenant Smith and fifteen comrades rode for help, arriving at Fort Rice four days later. Early on the morning of September 20, the emigrants spotted twenty to thirty horsemen on a ridge north of camp. They were the advance party of Colonel Daniel J. Dill, who was a few miles behind with 400 cavalry soldiers, 400 infantrymen, and a section of artillery from Fort Rice. The Hunkpapa warriors retreated, and the sixteen-day siege came to an end. The frightened gold seekers returned to Fort Rice, where the expedition disbanded.

A diary of the battle kept by William L. Larned describes the events and setting in

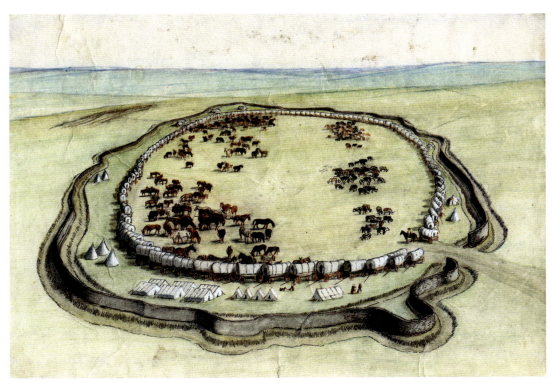

Hand-tinted pen-and-ink drawing of Fort Dilts, by Charles O. Miller, based on a sketch by H.H. Larned. SHSND 1992.0007

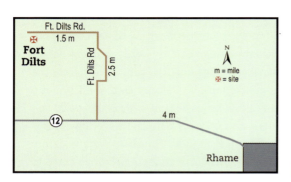

vivid detail, and many of the features are still visible, including the sod wall, wagon ruts, graves, and an uncompleted well. Archaeological excavations confirm the site is essentially undisturbed. A flagpole, a site marker, and several grave markers are present. ◄

▼▼▼▼▼▼▼▼▼▼▼▼▼▼▼▼▼▼

FROM RHAME, BOWMAN COUNTY
West 4 miles on ND-12 and north 2.5 miles and west 1.5 miles on Ft. Dilts Road. The site is marked by an aluminum plaque on a petrified wood marker south of the road.
GPS 46.279121, -103.776424

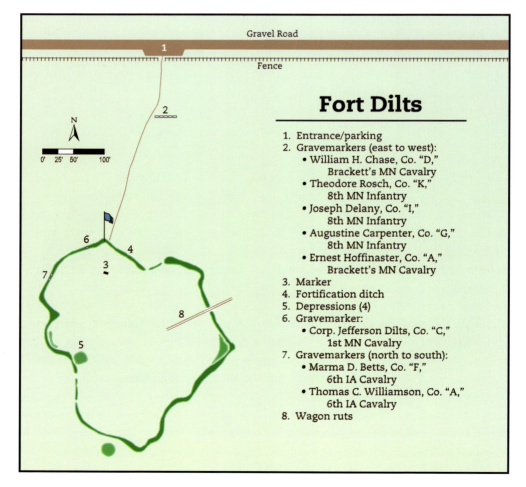

Fort Dilts

1. Entrance/parking
2. Gravemarkers (east to west):
   - William H. Chase, Co. "D," Brackett's MN Cavalry
   - Theodore Rosch, Co. "K," 8th MN Infantry
   - Joseph Delany, Co. "I," 8th MN Infantry
   - Augustine Carpenter, Co. "G," 8th MN Infantry
   - Ernest Hoffinaster, Co. "A," Brackett's MN Cavalry
3. Marker
4. Fortification ditch
5. Depressions (4)
6. Gravemarker:
   - Corp. Jefferson Dilts, Co. "C," 1st MN Cavalry
7. Gravemarkers (north to south):
   - Marma D. Betts, Co. "F," 6th IA Cavalry
   - Thomas C. Williamson, Co. "A," 6th IA Cavalry
8. Wagon ruts

Fort Mandan Overlook
STATE HISTORIC SITE

FORT MANDAN OVERLOOK is so named because the site overlooks the area where Lewis and Clark established their headquarters, called Fort Mandan, in the winter of 1804–1805. Fort Mandan was a triangular fort which provided shelter, protection, and a place of cultural interchange between the explorers and the area's Indian inhabitants, for whom the fort was named. The original site of Fort Mandan was beside the river and has been inundated.

In 1991–1992 State Historical Society archeologists excavated part of the site, which lies fourteen miles west of Washburn, McLean County, overlooking the Missouri River. Based on these studies, we now know that people lived at this location during two different times: once during the late-1700s to mid-1800s and earlier, around A.D. 1300 to 1400. An irregular ditch constructed sometime during the late-eighteenth century to mid-nineteenth century is the most visible feature at this archaeological site. At present no historic documents have been found that identify the date of construction of the ditch, the builders, or the events that transpired there. Historic-period artifacts found in the sod and just below it include glass trade beads, a gunflint, lead shot, and glass fragments.

Although the eighteenth- and nineteenth-century events at the site remain a puzzle, the prehistoric use is better understood. A significant Plains Village campsite (fourteenth century) was discovered by the archeologists.

While no houses were detected during excavation or are visible on the ground surface, contemporary Plains Villagers in the area lived in rectangular houses (see **Huff Indian Village**). Recovered artifacts include pottery, arrowheads, scrapers, flakes, grinding tools, bison shoulder-blade hoe fragment, butchered animal bones, and corn kernels and cobs. A pit filled with ash and a hearth were also uncovered. Charcoal from the hearth was radiocarbon dated to A.D. 1300 to 1400. Based on the archaeological excavations, inhabitants occupying the site more than six centuries ago were involved in such activities as food preparation, hide processing, and stone tool production and repair.

There are two markers at the site, one identifying it as a state historic site and the other placed there by the Masons. ◀

FROM JUNCTION 83 AND ND-200A AT WASHBURN, McLEAN COUNTY

South 0.1 mile on ND-200A, west 10.8 miles on 8th St. SW to a .6 mile curve to the north, and west and south 1.7 miles to the site access road. The site is marked by an aluminum plaque west of the road.
GPS 47.296306, -101.285137

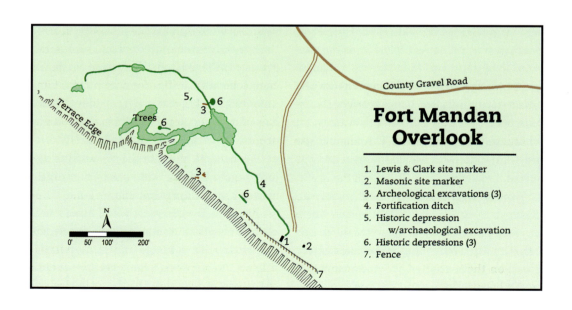

Fort Ransom STATE HISTORIC SITE

FORT RANSOM, established in 1867 to safeguard overland travel from Minnesota to Montana, was named in honor of brevet Major General Thomas E. G. Ransom of the US Volunteers. Today, although the building locations and the dry moat are still clearly discernible, nothing else remains of the original fort or its twelve-foot-high sod and log stockade. The historic site is located southwest of the town of Fort Ransom, Ransom County.

On June 17, 1867, a battalion of the 10th US Infantry, commanded by brevet Major George H. Crosman, arrived from Fort Wadsworth in southern Dakota Territory. Soldiers began work on enclosing a breastwork and completed it by August. Oak logs from the nearby Sheyenne River Valley were used to construct the post. The buildings were arranged within the earthen breastworks in a square, measuring 350 by 400 feet. Ten square miles around the fort were designated as Fort Ransom Military Reservation, Dakota Territory.

With the exception of two, all were one-story log buildings. The barracks building was under one roof on the north side of the square and was subdivided into four large rooms for the enlisted men and two small rooms for the first sergeants. Box stoves warmed quarters, and each squad room had three windows. Kitchens were attached to the rear of the quarters. Other buildings at the post were quartermaster and commissary storehouses, quarters for married men, a granary, bakery, guardhouse, hospital, office for commandant and adjutant, stables, and the magazine. Outside the breastworks were quarters for the Indian scouts.

Survival at this military post, like any frontier settlement, was a constant struggle. Water for drinking and cooking had to be hauled from a spring 600 yards away. Facilities for bathing at the post were limited, and the nearby river was used for that purpose during the summer. The vegetable garden, eight acres in size, was near the post, and hay for livestock was harvested three miles to the south.

Quartermaster teams linked Fort Abercrombie to Fort Ransom, and a tri-weekly coach ran to St. Cloud, Minnesota. In winter the route from Fort Ransom to Fort Abercrombie was particularly dangerous due to storms, and in spring, flooding on the Wild Rice River stopped communication. In good weather the weekly mail by horseback via Fort Abercrombie took eight days to reach St. Paul, Minnesota.

Fort Ransom was dismantled in 1872, and the materials were used to build Fort Seward at Jamestown, Stutsman County. The army had determined that protection of the Northern Pacific Railroad crew at the James River crossing was a higher priority than safeguarding the overland route. The final disposition of the military reservation took place on July 14, 1880, when it was turned over to the Department of the Interior for survey and sale to homesteaders.

Today a marker describing the military fort sits beside a parking area on the east side of a county road. Building remnants and cellars, a fortification ditch with an embankment, and a flagpole mark the remains of this once thriving post. ◀

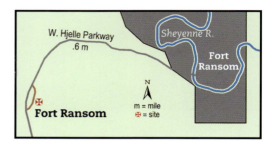

FROM FORT RANSOM, RANSOM COUNTY
West and south .6 mile on W. Hjelle Parkway. The site is east of the road.
GPS 46.518543, -97.941447

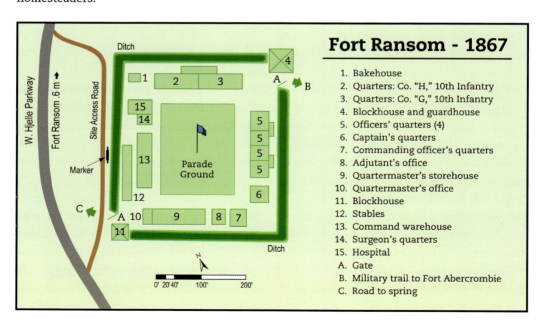

Fort Ransom - 1867

1. Bakehouse
2. Quarters: Co. "H," 10th Infantry
3. Quarters: Co. "G," 10th Infantry
4. Blockhouse and guardhouse
5. Officers' quarters (4)
6. Captain's quarters
7. Commanding officer's quarters
8. Adjutant's office
9. Quartermaster's storehouse
10. Quartermaster's office
11. Blockhouse
12. Stables
13. Command warehouse
14. Surgeon's quarters
15. Hospital
A. Gate
B. Military trail to Fort Abercrombie
C. Road to spring

Fort Rice STATE HISTORIC SITE

FORT RICE was established on July 7, 1864, by General Alfred H. Sully as a field base during his 1864 expedition. The fort was named for Brigadier General James Clay Rice of Massachusetts who was killed at the Battle of the Wilderness during the Civil War. Fort Rice was the first of a chain of forts intended to guard Northern Plains transportation routes, evidence of the United States government's changing policy toward these western lands, encouraging their settlement and providing protection for Euro-American settlers. Fort Rice became one of the most important military posts on the Upper Missouri River. It is located approximately thirty miles south of Mandan, Morton County.

During the summer of 1864, Sioux in Dakota Territory were angered by the military expeditions that had attacked Dakota, Lakota, and Yanktonai bands the previous year (see **Sibley's and Sully's Northwest Indian Campaigns**). In response, the Indians increased their attacks on Northern Plains transportation routes, including steamboats traveling on the Upper Missouri.

In 1864 General Sully returned to the Upper Missouri with an army of 3,500 men to punish the Sioux, to force them onto reservations, and to strengthen the peace by building military forts near the mouth of Long Lake Creek (Fort Rice), at the confluence of the Yellowstone and Missouri Rivers (eventually Fort Buford), and near the mouth of the Powder River. The army hired fifteen steamboats to transport men and supplies part of the distance and retained three steamboats to support the expedition for its four-month duration.

Sully's first action was to select a location

for Fort Rice. The military reservation for the fort covered approximately 175 square miles (112,000 acres) and was established by Executive Orders of September 2, 1864, and January 22, 1867. The first structures were built by several companies of the 30th Wisconsin Infantry under Colonel Daniel J. Dill. Cottonwood logs, cut from the wooded banks of the Missouri River, formed the stockade, 510 feet by 500 feet. Two log blockhouses, each twenty feet square, guarded the northeast and the southwest corners of the stockade. The fort buildings inside the stockade were built with cottonwood logs and had sod roofs.

In the autumn of 1864, six companies of the 1st US Volunteer Infantry arrived to replace the Wisconsin infantry. The "volunteers" were primarily Confederate prisoners of war, also called Galvanized Yankees. These prisoners enlisted in the Union Army to protect the western frontier rather than wait to be paroled or exchanged for Yankee prisoners of war, or be sent north to work on government fortifications. Two companies of the similarly organized 4th US Volunteers arrived as reinforcements in 1865. Upon the disbandment of the US Volunteers, these units were replaced by Union volunteer troops (state militia) and after the war by troops of the "regular" army.

Life was not easy in these small frontier forts, isolated by distance and a seasonally ice-bound transportation system. During the fort's first year, eighty-one men died—thirty-seven from scurvy, twenty-four from chronic diarrhea, three of typhoid fever, ten of other diseases, and seven killed in combat. To pass the time during the first winter, the soldiers opened a theater, and from June 15 through October 9, 1865, they published their own newspaper, the *Frontier Scout*.

Throughout its existence, Fort Rice was a highly active military post. It served as base of operations for General Sully's First and Sec-

Linda Warfel Slaughter drew this sketch of Fort Rice as it appeared in 1871, when she lived at the post with her husband, Frank Slaughter, the post surgeon. She settled in Bismarck and was an educator, journalist, historian, and women's rights advocate in North Dakota. *The Record, 06-1898, V 3, No 12, 233*

ond Northwestern Expeditions of 1864 and 1865. In 1866–1868, important Indian councils were held at the post. The most important of these was the Great Council with various Sioux bands in July 1868. Although a key leader of the Lakota, Tȟatȟáŋka Íyotake (Sitting Bull), refused to participate, Father Pierre Jean De Smet did convince Sitting Bull to allow his chief lieutenant, Phizí (Gall), to attend this council. As a result of this council, area

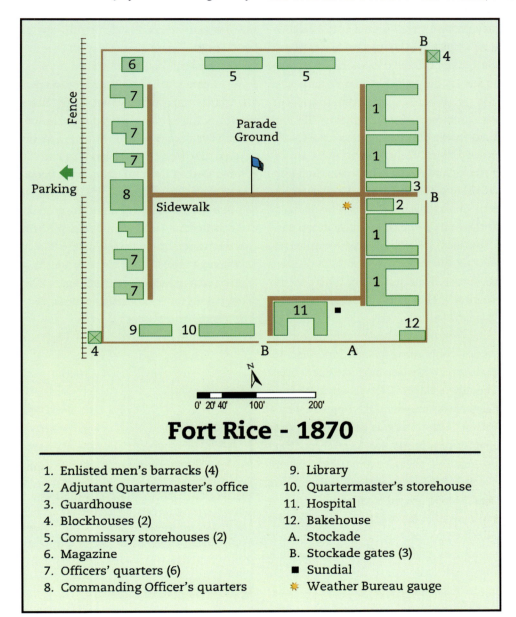

Fort Rice - 1870

1. Enlisted men's barracks (4)
2. Adjutant Quartermaster's office
3. Guardhouse
4. Blockhouses (2)
5. Commissary storehouses (2)
6. Magazine
7. Officers' quarters (6)
8. Commanding Officer's quarters
9. Library
10. Quartermaster's storehouse
11. Hospital
12. Bakehouse
A. Stockade
B. Stockade gates (3)
■ Sundial
✷ Weather Bureau gauge

Sioux bands signed the Fort Laramie Treaty of 1868, which ended the Red Cloud War and defined the boundaries of the Great Sioux Reservation. The reservation included most of the area west of the Missouri River in present-day South Dakota.

In 1868 Fort Rice was expanded to cover an area of 864 feet by 544 feet. It was protected by a ten-foot-high log stockade on three sides and by the Missouri River on the east. Within the stockade and surrounding the parade ground were four company barracks with kitchens, seven officers' quarters, a post hospital, bakery, storehouses, library, and a powder magazine. Outside the east line of buildings were the guardhouse and post headquarters. Various other buildings stood between these buildings and the stockade, such as company sinks (privies), laundress quarters, and bathhouse. Outside the stockade were the stables, barns, corrals, blacksmith shop, Indian scouts' quarters, and the post-trader's store.

The new barracks were made of pine lumber, but all other buildings were built from locally sawn cottonwood boards. Some were insulated with homemade adobe bricks stacked between the wall studs. Clapboard siding and shingled roofs completed the improvements.

Although the fort was designed for four companies of infantry, it was later modified to accommodate several companies of the 7th US Cavalry. While the average garrison was 235 men, troops ranged from a high of 357 in 1874 to a low of 61 in 1878. Throughout the history of the fort, the soldiers guarded against Indian attacks. Warriors assaulted haying and logging parties and raided the horse and cattle herds of the army and of civilian traders. These raids continued as late as 1877.

Between 1871 and 1873, Fort Rice served as the base for the three Yellowstone expeditions, which escorted parties surveying the route of the Northern Pacific Railroad. Four companies of the Fort Rice contingent of the 7th Cavalry accompanied Lieutenant Colonel George A. Custer on his Black Hills expedition in 1874. Two companies from Fort Rice fought in the Battle of the Little Bighorn.

The post was abandoned on November 25, 1878, after the establishment of Fort Yates on the Standing Rock Agency. In 1913 the State of North Dakota acquired Fort Rice, and in the 1940s, the Works Progress Administration (WPA) marked the foundations of many of the Fort Rice buildings.

None of the original buildings or structures remain at Fort Rice. Visitors will see depressions, foundation lines, and WPA corner markers. A brief history of the fort and a map appear on a site marker. Parking space is available, but there are no visitor services.

FROM FORT RICE, MORTON COUNTY
South .8 mile on ND-1806 to the site access road on the east side of the highway. The site is marked by an aluminum plaque and stone building corners east of the highway.
GPS 46.512999, -100.582972

Fort Stevenson STATE PARK

LOCATED ON Lake Sakakawea's north shore is Fort Stevenson State Park, named for a late-1800s military post. The original site of the fort, now underwater following the creation of Lake Sakakawea, was on the north bank of the Missouri River, about two miles southwest of the present park.

The original Fort Stevenson was established in 1867 to guard the emigrant route from Minnesota to the gold mines of Montana and Idaho. It also provided military protection from the Dakota for the Mandan, Arikara, and Hidatsa tribes settled at Like-a-Fishhook Village, located about eighteen miles upriver from Fort Stevenson. The post served as an intermediate point for the mail routes connecting the string of military posts across the Northern Plains and eventually became the supply base for Fort Totten, 126 miles to the east. The post consisted of ten rough buildings made from materials found in the area. Deterioration of the buildings began even before the post was completed, as bricks crumbled in hard rains and cottonwood shrank and warped as it dried.

An exceptional account of life at Fort Stevenson can be found in the writings of Philippe Regís de Trobriand, who commanded the fort from 1867 until 1870. Although the post itself was never attacked, war parties were sighted and mail messengers were sometimes attacked and killed. The military campaigns that followed Custer's defeat at the Little Bighorn ended the power of the Dakota, and Fort Stevenson was officially abandoned by the army in August 1883. The buildings were turned over to the Bureau of Indian Affairs and used as the Fort Berthold Indian School until 1894, and then later sold at public auction.

A replica of the fort's original guardhouse has been constructed by the Fort Stevenson Foundation and houses interpretive exhibits about the original fort and the Missouri River.

Fort Stevenson State Park's other major visitor attractions are its access to the Lake Sakakawea fishery and water sports, accessible through the two marinas located in the park. An arboretum containing more than fifty native and non-native trees, shrubs, wildflowers, and grasses is well established near the campgrounds. While a variety of birds and animals are found, there are two rare species to be seen, the black-tailed prairie dog and piping plover.

Fort Stevenson State Park's camping and picnicking facilities are open through the year. Showers, electrical hookups and a sewage dump station are available from Memorial Day through Labor Day. Small sleeping cabins can be rented during the summer months and are equipped with lights, heat, fan and deck. Special events are held throughout the summer as well as scheduled amphitheater presentations and other activities. There is a fee to enter the park.

Campground reservations can be made on the North Dakota Parks and Recreation Department website at www.parkrec.nd.gov or by calling (800) 827-4723. For more information about Fort Stevenson State Park, check the website or call the park at (701) 337-5576. ◂

Philippe de Trobriand during the Civil War, when he held the brevet rank of general. After the war he served at a number of western military posts, including Fort Stevenson, where he documented the harsh conditions faced by frontier soldiers. LC-B813-6803

A skilled artist, de Trobriand painted the winter quarters at Fort Stevenson as they appeared during the severe winter of 1867–68. SHSND 12470

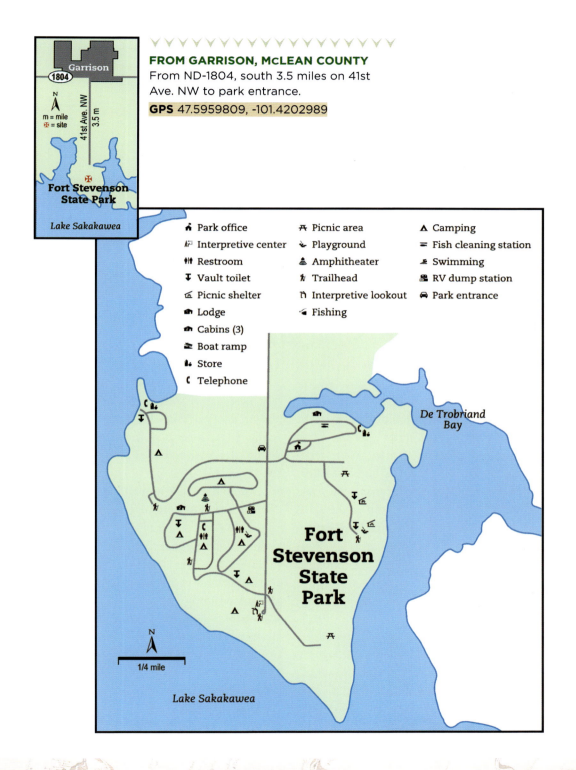

Fort Totten
STATE HISTORIC SITE

FORT TOTTEN is one of the best preserved frontier military posts in the United States because of its later use as an Indian boarding school. Sixteen of the original military structures still stand at the Fort Totten State Historic Site, located in the town of Fort Totten in Benson County on the Spirit Lake Nation Reservation boundaries. The area surrounding Devils Lake has been a gathering place for Dakota peoples for hundreds of years.

The fort was built between 1867 and 1873 as a military outpost, but for most of its history it served as a boarding school for Indian children. The original garrison policed the surrounding military reservation, guarded overland mail and transportation routes, and provided both protection and oversight for the Dakota Indians living on the Spirit Lake Nation Reservation. Military units stationed at the fort always included infantry soldiers, and various detachments of the famous Seventh US Cavalry were stationed at the post during the 1870s.

Decommissioned as a military post in December 1890, the buildings were transferred to the US Department of the Interior for use as an industrial boarding school for Indian children. The first students, aged from five to twenty-one years, were primarily from the surrounding Dakota reservation. They were later joined by Chippewa children from the Turtle Mountain Indian Reservation and others, until at one time the boarding school had the largest student body (more than 400) of any of the schools in the federal system. Students received vocational and academic training in such skills as seamstress/tailoring, harness and shoe making, baking, farming, dairying, printing, and carpentry.

The industrial boarding school closed in 1935 when Fort Totten became the site of a tuberculosis preventorium, a five-year experimental program that placed children considered at high risk for contracting tuberculosis in a closed, controlled environment that provided both care and education. At the end of the program in 1940, Fort Totten again became a combination day-school and boarding school, with increased involvement by the local Indian community in its operation. A new school was opened in 1959, and the historic site was abandoned. In 1960 the site was designated as a state historic site.

The original brick military structures around the parade ground are the adjutant's office, two first lieutenant's quarters, two second lieutenant's quarters, commanding officer's quarters, chaplain's and surgeon's quarters, hospital/chapel, commissary storehouse, quartermaster's storehouse, powder magazine, three company barracks, and a bakery. An ADA-accessible boardwalk guides visitors to Fort Totten on a tour of these buildings, beginning with an updated introductory exhibit and museum store in the Fort Totten

Fort Totten Indian Industrial School, circa 1910. SHSND A1525

Fort Totten circa 1910, during its use as an Indian boarding school. School activities included sports. Here, the 1913 girls basketball team poses for a photograph. SHSND 970.637 T641

Exhibits tell the story of life in the military and at the Indian school.

Interpretive Center. The Center is in the restored commissary storehouse (Building 23). The new exhibit describes the military, Indian school, and historic preservation activities at Fort Totten. The staff at Fort Totten State Historic Site place a strong emphasis on locating and recording the oral histories of as many former students and employees as possible. Oral histories are helping to better interpret this sometimes painful part of the history of this site.

While strolling around the parade ground, one can explore several structures open to the public or view window exhibit panels describing the functions of key buildings. Buildings painted gray with red trim display the original military color scheme. Buildings painted white with green trim show the post-1904 Indian school color scheme.

The company barracks/main school (Building 14) is the home of the present-day Fort Totten Little Theater, where a local musical theater group stages productions every July. An Indian school classroom display and artifacts from Plummer's Mercantile Store of Minnewaukan, North Dakota, are exhibited in this building, and vending machine concessions are available. The site supervisor's administrative office is here also.

A gymnasium (Building 13) replaced what was originally a fourth company barracks building. At the time of construction in 1925 it was noted as the largest school gymnasium in the state.

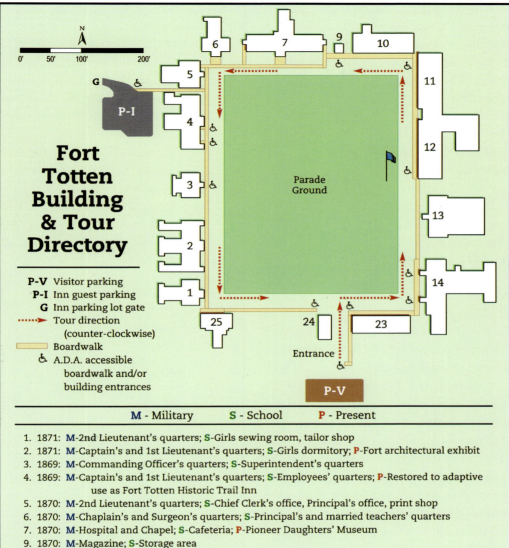

The company barracks/boys dormitory (Building 12) currently houses memorabilia from the North Dakota Odd Fellows/Rebekah Lodges. The first Odd Fellows lodge in what is now North Dakota was established in 1878 at the Fort Totten military post. Window exhibits also show the uses of the building as a military company barracks and as a boys dormitory. The adjoining company barracks/boys dormitory (Building 11) hosts traveling exhibits and features an audiovisual program about the history of Fort Totten. An interpretive exhibit is featured at the quartermaster's storehouse/bakery, laundry, and harness shop (Building 10). The powder magazine/school flour storage (Building 9) contains a display on the military use of the building. The hospital/school cafeteria (Building 7) is used by the Lake Region Pioneer Daughters as a museum. A window exhibit is located in the second lieutenant's quarters/principal's office and print shop (Building 5).

The larger officers' quarters/school employee residence (Building 4) has been restored to an adaptive use as the Totten Trail Historic Inn through a cooperative agreement with the Friends of Fort Totten Historic Site. Overnight stays are available seasonally in rooms furnished in period styles from 1870 to 1910. Other facilities are also available for meetings and receptions throughout the year. For information, call (701) 766-4874 or go to www.tottentrailinn.com.

The commanding officer's quarters, later the superintendent's quarters (Building 3), is partially restored and contains exhibits of life on "Officer's Row." Another officers' quarters/girls dormitory (Building 2) has been partially restored, and an interior boardwalk with an observation deck has been installed.

Fort Totten State Historic Site is listed on the National Register of Historic Places and is open year-round as an outdoor museum. Buildings are open to the public daily from May 16 through September 15. A fee is charged for admission to the site. State Historical Society of North Dakota Foundation members and children five and under are admitted free; school groups pay reduced admission.

For more information, contact the site supervisor, Fort Totten State Historic Site, P.O. Box 224, Fort Totten, North Dakota 58335, call (701) 766-4441, or visit the Society's web site.

AT FORT TOTTEN, BENSON COUNTY
From ND-57 at the edge of Devils Lake, south .9 mile on BIA Road-7. The site is located east of the road.
GPS 47.977667, -98.993238

Fort Union Trading Post
NATIONAL HISTORIC SITE

FROM 1828 TO 1867, Fort Union dominated the fur trade on the Upper Missouri River. Built near the confluence of the Yellowstone and Missouri Rivers by John Jacob Astor's powerful American Fur Company, the post controlled the trading economy of the Northern Plains. Much of the fort's early success was due to Scottish-born Kenneth McKenzie, who supervised the construction of the post and served as the post's first bourgeois, or superintendent. Under his leadership, the fort soon became headquarters for trading beaver pelts and buffalo hides with the Assiniboines, Crows, Crees, Ojibwas, Hidatsas, and Blackfeet Indians. Fort Union was part of a series of trading posts, including **Fort Clark,** constructed along the Missouri River.

Fort Union stood on a grassy plain that provided space for Indian camps at trading time. A palisade of vertical logs enclosed a quadrangle 220 feet by 140 feet, and two-story stone bastions at two of the corners were used as observation posts. Employees occupied rooms in a long building on the west side of the interior. A similar building on the east side contained a retail store and storerooms for furs, meat, and trade goods. At the north end stood the imposing bourgeois house, and behind it, a bell tower and kitchen.

In its heyday, Fort Union employed up to 100 men, many of whom were married to Indian women and had families living with them. Starting with Kenneth McKenzie, Fort Union witnessed a succession of strong bourgeois, including Alexander Culbertson and Edwin Denig. Other important members of the fort's staff were the clerks, responsible for maintaining inventories of trade goods, furs and hides, and other items. Another key group was the interpreters, who had to know several Indian languages as well as English and French. Hunters, often men of mixed blood, supplied the tables with fresh meat—buffalo, elk, or deer. Traders sent to Indian camps during the winter returned in the spring, preferably with a load of furs and no leftover trade goods.

A wide range of visitors came to Fort Union, including adventurers, scientists, artists, and priests. One of the first visitors, artist George Catlin, arrived in 1832 on board the *Yellow Stone*, the first Upper Missouri steamboat to reach the fort. Prince Maximilian of Wied, Father Pierre De Smet, John James Audubon, Karl Bodmer, and Rudolph Frederick Kurz were among other early visitors who made paintings of the fort or wrote vivid accounts of life there. Some company employees, such as Edwin Denig, also engaged in ethnographic study.

When McKenzie established Fort Union, beaver had been in great demand for nearly three decades. By the early 1830s the demand for beaver skins began to decline as the market for tanned buffalo robes increased. Coupled with improved river transportation, the buffalo robe trade caused the fort to flourish. In 1837, however, the steamboat *St. Peters* arrived at Fort Union, bringing smallpox with it. The disease struck the fort's employees and spread to the Assiniboines, who had little resistance to the foreign virus. Out of the approximately 1000 people in the band who caught the disease, only about 150 survived. The Blackfeet were also ravaged by the disease.

By the early 1850s, when the buffalo trade was at its height, about 25,000 buffalo robes were shipped out of Fort Union each year.

Fort Union in 1853, as depicted by John Mix Stanley, artist for the railroad survey expedition led by Isaac J. Stevens. SHSND C0633

Signs of coming change, however, were apparent on the upper Missouri. While buffalo herds were still immense, white civilization was beginning to encroach on the homelands of the Plains Indians. Further epidemics reduced populations and trade. The Sioux, who had lived further downstream, were forced by white expansion to roam westward in increasing numbers and were becoming hostile. By the time the Civil War began, trade in general had declined and the post was in need of repair. After the US-Dakota War of 1862 in Minnesota, the US Army undertook campaigns against the Dakota that led to the establishment of Fort Buford nearby. Fort Union was sold to the Army in 1867 and the buildings were dismantled and used to expand Fort Buford.

By the 1920s both the State Historical Society of North Dakota and the Great Northern Railroad had expressed an interest in reconstructing Fort Union. The Society acquired title to the property in 1938 and later passed it to the National Park Service which, between 1985 and 1991, reconstructed portions of Fort Union Trading Post to their 1851 appearance, including the walls, stone bastions, Indian trade house, and Bourgeois House.

An interpreter in period clothing stands in the Indian trade house.

Fort Union Trading Post National Historic Site is open year-round except for winter holidays. The facilities at the site include exhibits about life at Fort Union, a video program, a book store, restrooms, and concession machines. During the summer the trade house is occupied by an interpreter in period clothing. Hours are 8:00 A.M. to 6:30 P.M. Central Time Memorial Day through Labor Day, and from 9:00 A.M. to 5:30 P.M. Central Time Labor Day to Memorial Day. For more information write the superintendent, Fort Union Trading Post NHS, 15550 HWY 1804, Williston, North Dakota 58801, call (701) 572-9083, or go to the internet site www.nps.gov/fous. ◄

FROM BUFORD, WILLIAMS COUNTY
West 2.5 miles on ND-1804 and south .2 mile to the site parking area. The site is a 5-minute walk east on a paved trail.
GPS 47.9991667, -104.0425

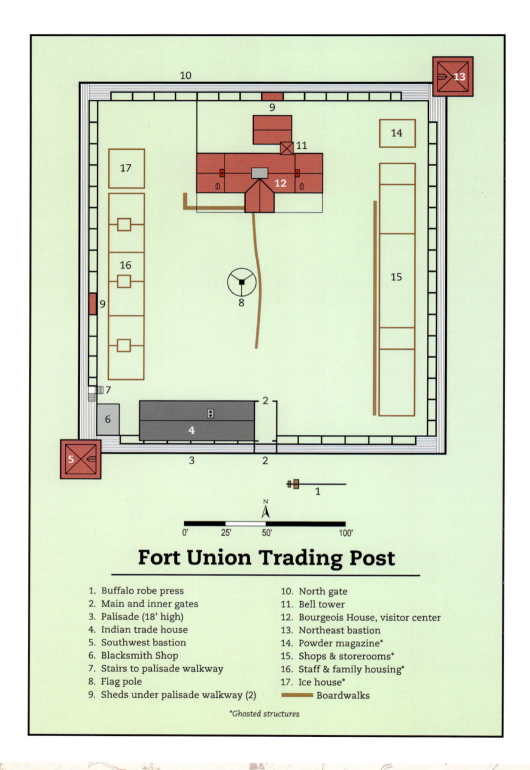

Gingras Trading Post
STATE HISTORIC SITE

THE GINGRAS TRADING POST State Historic Site preserves the 1840s home and trading post of Métis legislator and businessman Antoine Blanc Gingras, northeast of Walhalla, Pembina County. Métis, meaning "mixed blood" or "mixed race," is a term used by people of combined Indian and European ancestry to describe themselves. Gingras was a prominent fur trader, who in 1861 claimed a net worth of $60,000 and later increased his holdings to include a chain of trading posts extending across northern Dakota Territory and southern Manitoba. Gingras's hand-hewn oak log store and home are among the few tangible remains of the fur trade in the Red River Valley.

Antoine B. Gingras was significant in the history of the region. In 1851 he was elected to serve in the Minnesota Territorial House of Representatives. He participated in the 1869 rebellion led by Louis Riel against the government of Manitoba to gain a national homeland and self-government for the Métis people. Gingras also took part in chartering the City of Winnipeg.

Both buildings on Gingras State Historic Site have been restored to their original appearance. While logs are exposed on the two-story trading post, clapboard siding covers the log structure of the house. The siding was added soon after the house was built. The house has been painted in its original his-

SHSND 200-4x5-0282

toric colors, as determined by study of traces of the original paint. The exterior is deep red with white trim, and the interior reproduces the original color scheme of blue walls, yellow floors, pink ceilings, and green and brown trim. Interpretive panels and exhibits about Gingras, Métis heritage, and the fur trade are located in the restored house. Outside the buildings are interpretive signs and panels. Authentic reproductions of fur trade goods are sold in the Gingras store.

The site is listed on the National Register of Historic Places and is open from 10:00 to 5:00 daily, May 16 through September 15. Admission is free, and donations are accepted. For more information during the summer season, contact Gingras State Historic Site, 12882 105th Street NE, Walhalla, North Dakota, 58282, or call (701) 549-2775. Information may be obtained year round by contacting the Pembina State Museum at (701) 825-6840. ◄

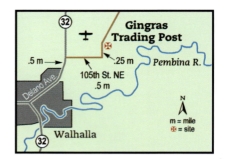

FROM WALHALLA, PEMBINA COUNTY
North .5 mile on ND-32, east .5 mile and north .25 mile on 105th St. NE. The site is marked by a sign and two buildings east of the road.
GPS 48.936907, -97.890866

A Métis family with their Red River carts, 1883. SHSND A4365

Hudson Townsite STATE HISTORIC SITE

THE HUDSON TOWNSITE State Historic Site, southwest of Oakes in Dickey County, marks the location of one of many speculative townsites established during the Great Dakota Boom (1879–1886) by people who hoped they could attract one or more railroads. This townsite is an example of the boom-bust settlement typical of the time. The plan to establish a town called Hudson began in 1883 with the formation of the Dakota Midland Railroad. A group of promoters headed by W.H. Becker met in Ellendale, Dakota Territory, where they organized the railroad, obtained a charter, secured right-of-way, and projected several townsites, including Hudson. The neophyte railroad would extend from Ellendale through Hudson to Wahpeton.

The townsite plat for Hudson was printed and widely circulated by M.N. Chamberlain, one of the promoters, who quickly settled down in the new town to sell land. The original town plat shows thirty blocks divided into twenty-five and fifty-foot lots, a central town square, where prospective buyers might envision a magnificent city hall, and extensive railroad depot grounds at the north end of town. The James River, with a projected ferry crossing, ran along the eastern edge of town.

The 1884 *Andreas Historical Atlas* lists two hotels, three stores, three real estate and loan offices, a printing office, newspaper, livery stable, pump shop, blacksmith shop, and post office in the fledgling town. The newspaper, the *Hudson Herald*, was established on December 14, 1883, by R.S. Busteed. A combination school and church building was erected in 1885.

During the spring and summer of 1886, enthusiasm for the townsite died when the

Chicago and Northwestern Railroad pushed north to Oakes and laid its tracks on the east side of the James River opposite Hudson. That same year, the Northern Pacific Railroad ran a branch line to Oakes. The next year the Sault Ste. Marie Railroad acquired portions of the Dakota Midland's grade and pushed west into Oakes, bypassing Hudson.

As soon as the ice froze on the James in the winter of 1886–1887, the town of Hudson was picked up and moved to Oakes. Buildings were placed on skids and dragged by horses and oxen across the ice. The few buildings remaining in Hudson were torn down for lumber or left to disintegrate. In less than three years, a town was born, boomed, and vanished. All that remains are faint depressions, piles of stones, and a few artifacts. The Hudson townsite was acquired by the State Historical Society in 1936. The marker was dedicated July 15, 1956.

The Hudson townsite is also near the July 17, 1839, camp site of the John C. Frémont and Joseph Nicolas Nicollet expedition, early geographers who explored water courses in the Northwest. ◀

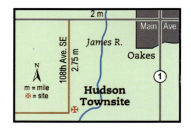

FROM OAKES, DICKEY COUNTY
West 2 miles on Main Street and south 2.75 miles on 108th Ave. SE. The site is marked by an aluminum plaque and a building depression east of the road.
GPS 46.096, -98.131404

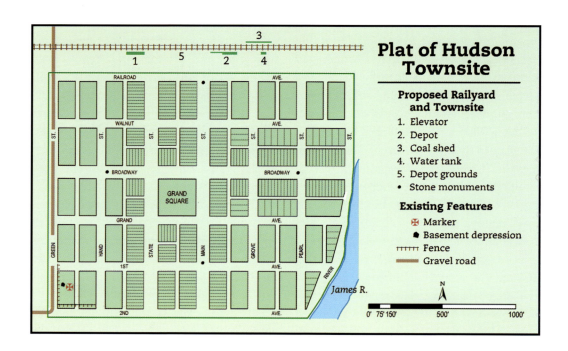

Huff Indian Village STATE HISTORIC SITE

HUFF INDIAN VILLAGE State Historic Site was a large prehistoric village that sheltered a population of approximately 1,000 people who were ancestors of the Mandan Indians in about A.D. 1450. It has been the focus of archaeological interest because of its large size and distinctive fortification system. The village is relatively pristine, and unlike many others in the state, it has never been cultivated. Remains of collapsed rectangular dwellings, which appear as oval or rectangular sunken depressions, and a fortification ditch are preserved at the site, located about twenty miles south of Mandan and one-half mile south of Huff, Morton County. Huff Indian Village is listed on the National Register of Historic Places as a National Historic Landmark.

The unusual fortification that protected the village from attack featured ten bastions spaced at regular intervals providing an impressive defense of the village. The dry moat (ditch) was fifteen feet wide, between two feet and five feet deep, and had a line of outward pointing stakes mounted on its inner edge. When the ditch was constructed, excavated soil was thrown toward the inside where it formed a distinct, low ridge. The fortification enclosed an eight-acre rectangular area containing at least 103 house depressions, although originally it may have been more than ten acres in size with 115 houses. The east side of the site facing the river was protected by a steep bank.

Archaeological excavations reveal that the houses were predominantly long, rectangular buildings. Multiple fireplaces within the houses suggest that the homes were occupied by several extended families (multiple generations or close relatives), each with its own fireplace. The houses were roughly aligned in rows, with the entrances facing to the southwest, away from the river.

An exceptionally large house, located in the approximate center of the village, faced southwest toward a large, open area similar to the ceremonial plaza of historic Mandan villages. This building may have served as the village's ceremonial lodge. Archaeological excavations from the building remain open, leaving conspicuous hollows showing the locations of the house entryway, central hearth, storage pits, and post holes from the building's structural framework.

From A.D. 1100 to 1400, small settlements were broadly distributed along the Missouri River and other major streams in the state. Later (A.D. 1400–1600), there were fewer villages, but they were large, heavily fortified, compact sites such as Huff. Village density was about two to four houses per acre at the earlier sites but rose to approximately twelve houses per acre at Huff, where a much larger population resided. The consolidated and highly fortified villages show that a hostile environment threatened these horticulturists, although the identity of foes of the Huff

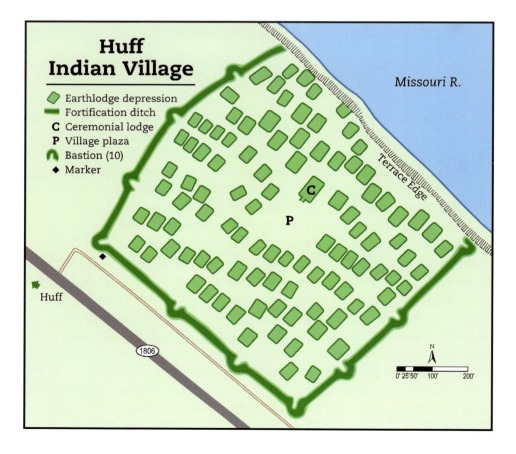

Detail of artist's rendition of the prehistoric village at Huff. Painting by Leon Basler

villagers is unknown. Factors for increased hostilities could have been the weakening of the small village groups by drought combined with increasing raids by nomads and, perhaps, competing downriver village groups.

By about the sixteenth century, the Mandan settlements changed from villages of long, rectangular houses, such as at Huff, to highly compact settlements of smaller, circular earthlodges, such as On-A-Slant Village at **Fort Abraham Lincoln State Park** (see also **Molander Indian Village** and **Double Ditch Indian Village**). The reason for the change is unknown, but motivating factors may have been conservation of building materials, heating efficiency, and influence from the Arikaras, who lived in circular earthlodges (see **Fort Clark**).

Archeologists excavated portions of the village in 1938–1939, 1959, and 1960, prior to increased erosion by Lake Oahe. In all, eleven houses and two bastions were investigated, resulting in the recovery of thousands of artifacts and, more importantly, providing scientific information about the inhabitants of this ancient site. An interpretive marker with a map stands near the entrance gate and other interpretive signs at the site provide additional information. ◄

AT HUFF, MORTON COUNTY
The site is east of ND-1806, just south of the town of Huff. Access is by way of a dirt road.
GPS 46.618568, -100.642512

Icelandic State Park

THE 912-ACRE Icelandic State Park's rich resources touch on geology, nature, history, and archaeology. Located five miles west of Cavalier on the north shore of Lake Renwick, the park includes the Pioneer Heritage Center and the Gunlogson Nature Preserve.

The Pioneer Heritage Center's exhibits feature efforts to homestead in the area between 1870 and 1920. During these years, immigrants from twenty-two countries settled in northeastern North Dakota, including the Icelanders, for whom the park was named. The original Gunlogson farmstead, listed on the National Register of Historic Places, can be toured, along with the Cranley School, Akra Hall, Hallson Church, and a replica log cabin. G.B. Gunlogson, whose parents settled property along the Tongue River in 1880, recognized the important natural significance of the wooded area along the river and donated 200 acres to the state in 1963 to become North Dakota's first dedicated state nature preserve.

Icelandic State Park is situated in the bed of glacial Lake Agassiz. Much of the land is heavily forested, with bottomland, hardwood, upland oak, and aspen/oak forest communities represented. Numerous plants and animals are present, with more than twenty rare species existing in the preserve.

Campfire programs, historical tours, environmental education, and guided nature walks are available at the park. A self-guided trail system is established along the Tongue River, with access beginning near the homestead site. Lake Renwick offers swimming, fishing, camping, and boating. A boat ramp, fishing dock, and a popular, gently sloping swim beach are located east of the camping area. Three modern campgrounds, a primitive campground, and walk-in tent sites are available.

During the winter, trails are groomed and tracked for cross-country skiing. A portion of the State Snowmobile Trail runs through the park, and Lake Renwick provides opportunities for ice fishing. A sledding hill can be found near the park's primitive campground.

Icelandic State Park's camping and picnicking facilities are open throughout the year, weather permitting. Hot showers, electrical hookups, and a sewage dump station are available from mid-May through the end of September. Campsites can be reserved by calling (800) 807-4723 or at the park's website, www.parkrec.nd.gov. For more information about Icelandic State Park, visit the website or call the park directly at (701) 265-4561. ◀

FROM CAVALIER, PEMBINA COUNTY
West 5.6 miles on ND-5. The park entrance is on the north side of the highway.
GPS 48.7611122, -97.9482885

Exhibits in the Pioneer Heritage Center feature homesteading in the area between 1870 and 1920.

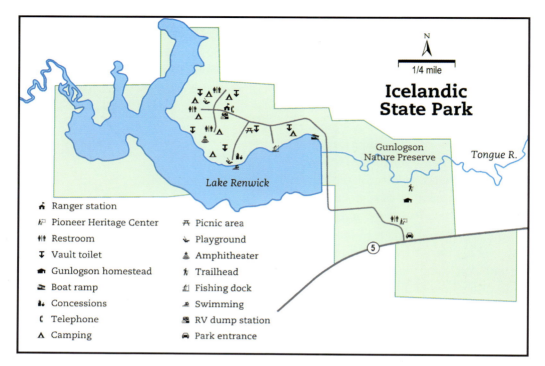

The trail system winds through the heavily forested park land.

International Peace Garden

THE INTERNATIONAL PEACE GARDEN, a picturesque symbol of peace between nations, rests on the world's longest unfortified border. Since 1932, this dazzlingly colorful botanical garden between Manitoba and North Dakota has welcomed visitors from all over the world. More than 150,000 flowers, including garden displays of the Canadian and American flags, are interspersed between seven peace poles, on which "May Peace Prevail" is written in twenty-eight different languages. Also at the site is a 120-foot Peace Tower and a Peace Chapel, along with steel girders brought from New York's World Trade Center at the 9/11 Memorial. Other popular features include a floral clock display, fountains, formal gardens, and terraced walkways.

Dedicated on July 14, 1932, the International Peace Garden was developed largely by the Civilian Conservation Corps under the direction of the National Park Service. Garden clubs and horticulturalists throughout the US and Canada have made generous contributions to the Peace Garden over the years, donating trees, plants, and seeds as well as maintenance and garden design work.

The sunken garden area was restored in 2009, and several thousand new trees, shrubs perennials and bulbs were planted, including a very diverse collection of hardy shrub roses.

The 9/11 site is being developed further to include a contemplative and stroll garden, as well as a recently completed Interpretive Center and Conservatory. The garden renovation and building construction was funded by the State of North Dakota, the Province of Manitoba, and the federal government of Canada while the 9/11 Memorial work is funded by Rotary International and the International Association of Fire Fighters.

Scenic hiking trails and auto tours wind through the verdant Turtle Mountain forests and pass the pristine waters of Lake Udall and Lake Stormon. Moose, deer, beaver, and a wide variety of birds and other wildlife roam the wildflowers, trees, shrubs, fountains, and formal gardens of the site. A modern campground is located in a wooded area near the CCC lodge, which is listed on the National Register for Historic Buildings. Garden tours, an interpretive center, café, and gift shop are available in the summer, while other outdoor activities can be enjoyed year-round.

Conventions, bus tours, weddings, receptions, reunions, socials, and camps fill the park each summer. The International Music Camp opened in 1956 with 116 students and eighteen instructors. Today, more than 2,800 students each summer study band, orchestra, ballet, piano, creative writing, organ performance, and fine arts under the direction of a diverse international faculty.

Located north of Dunseith at the northern terminus of US Route 281, the International Peace Garden is open to the public twenty-four hours per day, seven days a week with most visitor services open from late May through mid-September. There is an admission fee. Visitors must pass through US or Canadian customs on leaving the International Peace Garden. US citizens traveling to the site from within the United States will not be required to present a Western Hemisphere Travel Initiative-compliant document when exiting the park southbound. For more information, contact the International Peace Garden, R.R. 1, Box 116, Dunseith, North Dakota, 58329, or www.peacegarden.com.

The entrance to the International Peace Garden is located directly on the border between the United States and Canada. In addition to acres of gardens, walkways, and other features, there are also hiking trails and auto tours through the forests and around lakes like Lake Stormon (previous page).

FROM DUNSEITH, ROLETTE COUNTY

North 13.5 miles on US-281. The garden entrance is on the west side of the highway. Visitors must stop at US Customs upon leaving the park and returning to the US.

GPS 48.999268, -100.05455

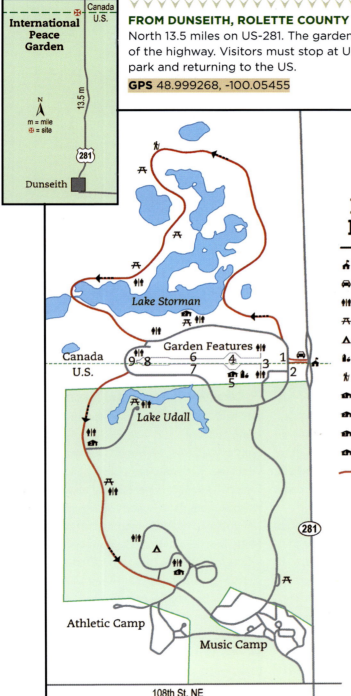

International Peace Garden

- US / Canadian Customs
- Site entrance
- Restroom
- Picnic area
- Camping
- Concessions
- Trailhead
- Interpretive center
- Errick Willis Pavilion
- Game Warden Museum
- Historic lodge
- One-way roads

Garden Features

1. Cairn
2. Floral clock
3. Formal garden
4. Sunken garden
5. Interpretive center
6. Carillion Bell Tower
7. 9/11 Memorial
8. Peace Tower
9. Peace Chapel

Killdeer Mountain Battlefield
STATE HISTORIC SITE

KILLDEER MOUNTAIN Battlefield State Historic Site overlooks the site of a battle fought on July 28, 1864, between troops commanded by General Sully and a gathering of Sioux Indians. This attack on an Indian trading village in the Killdeer Mountains was one of a series of military reprisals against the Sioux that followed the US-Dakota War of 1862 in Minnesota. However, many of the village's inhabitants were not involved in that war. The Killdeer Mountain Battlefield is eight and one-half miles northwest of Killdeer, Dunn County.

The region of Killdeer Mountain was long recognized as a good hunting spot and a gathering and trading point for groups of Sioux people. By July 1864 large numbers of Hunkpapas (including the chiefs Sitting Bull and Gall), some Sans Arcs, Miniconjous, and Blackfeet had arrived. Many Yanktonai people and a small number of Dakotas, some led by Inkpaduta, had also gathered.

On the afternoon of July 26, 1864, General Sully, with 2,200 troops supported by two artillery batteries, left a wagon train at the Heart River and began a march to the village (see **Sully's Heart River Corral**). That afternoon, military scouts fought a brief skirmish with a scouting party of Indians, but the troops pushed on.

On July 28 scouts raced back to the column and told Sully that they had found an Indian camp of about 1,500 lodges a few miles ahead. Sully immediately rearranged the marching order of the command into a huge, hollow square. Inside the square were his artillery, transport wagons, ambulances, and the command staff. Much of the cavalry dismounted to fight on foot. Every fourth man took the reins of his mount and three other horses and waited inside the square until needed. Tȟatȟáŋka Ská (White Bull), a Minniconjou Lakota who was present at the village that morning, later described Sully's formation as a mile-wide line of soldiers on foot, with other soldiers following on horseback, and a string of wagons following them.

After advancing four or five miles, the army confronted the Indians. Stories differ about who fired the first shot. White Bull described the battle as starting when a warrior named Šuŋká Išnála (Lone Dog) moved close to the soldiers' lines to see if they would shoot at him. Lone Dog was described by White Bull as being "with a ghost" or having a charm that made it difficult to shoot at him.[13] Lt. Col. John Pattee of the Seventh Iowa Cavalry described a similar event: "About this time an Indian, very gaily dressed, carrying a large war club gorgeously ornamented, appeared in front of the 6th Iowa Cavalry and called loudly to us and gesticulated wildly from about half a mile away. Major Wood, chief of cavalry, approached my position and said, 'The general sends his compliments and wishes for you to kill that Indian for God's sake.'"[14]

As the soldiers continued their advance toward the Indian encampment, groups of Indian warriors rode along the formation's flanks, skirmishing with the soldiers as they went, and circling around to the rear. At one point, cannons were brought forward to fire upon onlookers on a prominent hill, which stood squarely in the line's advance. At another point, an Indian scouting party, returning to the village, threatened the supply wagons at the rear until cannon were rushed back. Foot by foot, the soldiers advanced, and inch by inch, the Indians yielded.

As the day wore on General Sully ordered a cavalry charge to break the Indian line and drive it into forested breaks in front of and beside the village. Sergeant Eugene Marshall of Brackett's Cavalry would describe the charge as a "succession of hand-to-hand encounters, which ended in the death of one or the other party."[15]

Meanwhile, cannons reached a position overlooking the village. From this vantage point, cannons tore apart the village and the Indians' forward lines. The troops surrounded the village on three sides and advanced toward the center. More cannon began shelling the Indians out of the forested gullies behind the village and onto the exposed hillsides. Seeing that they no longer had any chance of repelling the troops, the Indians fled over the steep, rugged terrain to the rear. As their families climbed to safety, the warriors valiantly defended them until darkness silenced the guns. Oral traditions say some of the people escaped by climbing to the top of Killdeer Mountain and then down through a cave known today as the Medicine Hole.

The following morning, Sully left some of his troops at the village site to collect and destroy all abandoned materials. Col. Robert McLaren of the 2nd Minnesota Cavalry made a record of the destruction. He estimated that the soldiers burned about 1,400 lodges. "The men gathered into heaps and burned tons of dried buffalo meat packed in skin cases, great quantities of dried berries, buffalo robes, tanned buffalo, elk, and antelope skins, household utensils, such as brass and copper kettles, mess pans, etc., riding saddles and dray poles for ponies and dogs."[16] In his report after the battle, General Sully estimated that between 100 and 150 Indians were killed. No prisoners were taken. Lt. David Kingsbury of the 8th Minnesota Infantry would later recount that at least one infant was found alive in the abandoned village and subsequently shot.[17]

With the rest of his force, Sully set out after the people who had escaped Killdeer, but they made good use of the broken terrain, and Sully was unable to find them. Returning to the destroyed village, Sully gathered all his troops and marched back to Sully's Heart Corral. That night warriors attacked the picket line, killing two soldiers.

Survivors of the Battle of Killdeer Mountain still had some time before the onset of winter to replace some of their belongings. However, the battle solidified the antagonism of those Natives Americans, especially the Lakotas, who had not participated in the US-Dakota War of 1862, toward the encroaching whites.

The modern-day site bears considerable resemblance to the historic battlefield, despite modern intrusions of roads, fences, farms and ranches, and oil wells and collection facilities. Set against the scenic backdrop of the Killdeer Mountains, a sandstone slab monument and flagpole mark part of the July 28, 1864, battlefield. Two headstones honor soldiers who were killed in the cavalry charge. An unpaved parking lot is separated from the site by a log barrier. The one-acre site is surrounded by private land, so please be respectful. ◄

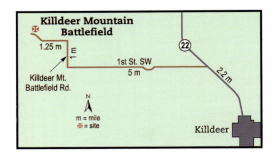

FROM KILLDEER, DUNN COUNTY
North 2.2 miles on ND-22, west 5 miles on 1st St. SW, and north 1 mile and west 1.25 miles on Killdeer Mt. Battlefield Road. The site is marked by an aluminum plaque north of the road.
GPS 47.421706, -102.916709

Looking toward the battlefield from near the top of Kildeer Mountain. The village was at the base of the hill at right, with the US Army attacking from the left side of this photo.

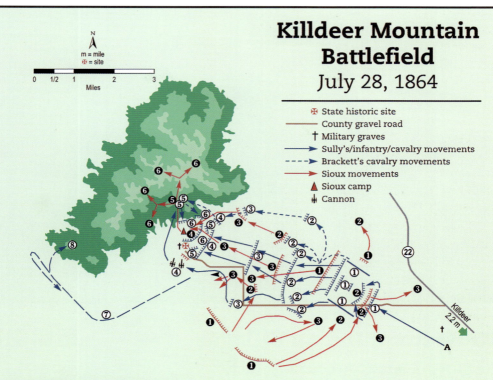

Killdeer Mountain Battlefield
July 28, 1864

A Sully approaches from the southeast.
① Sully's forces form a phalanx, advance across a flat plain toward higher ground to the west.
❶ Sioux confront the phalanx on the front and flanks.
❷ Sioux attack the phalanx from the front and rear, abandon flanks.
② Rear guard of phalanx confronts Sioux; forward section of phalanx presses Sioux line back; Brackett's Cavalry breaks towards the northwest to flank the Sioux.
❸ Sioux abandon advance on rear guard, probe south flank; forward line retreats slowly toward village.
③ Sully's forces continue a steady advance; Brackett confronts Sioux at eastern foothills.
❹ Sioux retreat to village.
④ Sully's forces begin to encircle the village, artillery flanks the village from the south and begins shelling.
❺ Sioux begin to abandon the village.
⑤ Sully's forward line continues to envelope the village, Brackett and other forces move around to rear of village to cut off Sioux retreat.
❻ Sioux retreat into Killdeer Mountain ravines, then into the badlands to the west.
⑥ Brackett and outlying forces return to join Sully's encirclement of the village.
⑦ July 29, 1864—Sully skirts the mountain trying to cut off the Sioux retreat—remaining troops destroy the village.
⑧ Sully's July 29th observation post.

Knife River Indian Villages
NATIONAL HISTORIC SITE

LOCATED JUST NORTH of the town of Stanton, the Knife River Indian Villages National Historic Site borders both sides of the Knife River directly north of its confluence with the Missouri River. For centuries this region of the Upper Missouri River was a center for agricultural settlement and trade. This archaeological park contains the remains of three historically important settlements established by ancestors of the modern Hidatsa Indian peoples, along with less-visible sites including older villages, trails, cemeteries, and a linear mound complex. In addition, there are more than fifty primary archaeological sites and villages within the 1,800-acre unit, many documenting the more than 10,000-year occupation of this bountiful landscape.

Of the three large villages, *Awatixa Xi'e*, or Lower Hidatsa Village, is the oldest, preserving the remains of about sixty earthlodges rebuilt many times over a period of 250 years. When the Hidatsas abandoned Lower Hidatsa Village, they eventually resettled at nearby *Awatixa* (Sakakawea Village) around 1795 and lived there in about forty lodges until 1834. Big Hidatsa Village was established by the "People of the Willows" around A.D. 1600, when this subgroup of the Hidatsa tribe moved upriver after living for a time with the Mandans at the Heart River. Big Hidatsa Village is the largest settlement in the park, with visible remains of 113 earthlodges, as well as travois trails.

Agriculture was the economic foundation of the Knife River people and the responsibility of the women of the tribe, who harvested much of their food from rich floodplain gardens. These proficient women farmers raised squash, pumpkin, beans, sunflowers, and quick-maturing varieties of corn. The villagers traded their surplus produce and Knife River flint to nomadic tribes for buffalo hides, deer skins, dried meat, catlinite (pipestone) and other items in short supply. Knife River flint was a prized material for making various stone tools, and was quarried locally. At the junction of major trade routes, the Hidatsas and Mandans became middlemen, dealing in goods from a vast network: obsidian from Wyoming, copper from the Great Lakes, shells from the Gulf of Mexico and the Pacific Northwest, and, after the seventeenth century, guns, horses, and metal items.

After centuries as a major trade center for American Indians, the Knife River Indian Villages became an important marketplace for British and French fur traders. The villages were also a destination for Lewis and Clark, who built their 1804–05 winter post, Fort Mandan, nearby. It was at one of these villages that Lewis and Clark met and hired the French fur trader Toussaint Charbonneau who, with his young wife Sakakawea, served as an interpreter on the journey to the Pacific Coast. Sakakawea would prove to be of great assistance on the expedition.

The years following the Lewis and Clark expedition brought many other traders and explorers, including Prince Maximilian of Wied and artists Karl Bodmer and George Catlin. New diseases also followed the traders to the Knife River villages, including a devastating smallpox epidemic in 1837 in which almost half the Hidatsa people and perhaps 90 percent of the residents of nearby Mandan villages died. The survivors abandoned the Knife River Village sites and moved north to create a new village called Like-a-Fishhook along the Missouri River.

Knife River Indian Villages National Historic Site is administered by the National Park

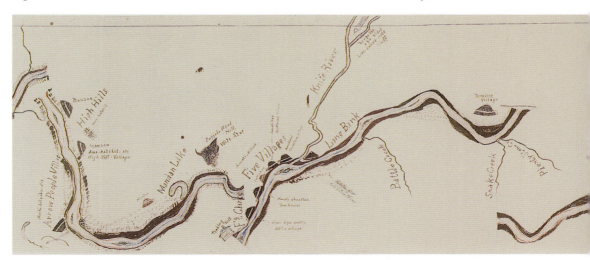

In 1905 a Mandan man, I-ki-ha-wa-he (Sitting Rabbit), created a map of the Mandan villages that had existed along the Missouri River, including this image of the villages by the Knife River. SHSND 679.

Service, US Department of the Interior. A visitor center with a movie, exhibits, and a bookstore is located at the site, which also features nature and historic trails through the major village sites and a reconstructed earthlodge. Hours are 8 A.M. to 6 P.M. (CT) Memorial Day through Labor Day, 8 A.M. to 4:30 P.M. (CT) the rest of the year. Admission is free. For more information, contact the park, P.O. Box 9, Stanton, ND 58571-0009, call (701) 745-3300, or go to the web site www.nps.gov/knri. ◄

▼▼▼▼▼▼▼▼▼▼▼▼▼▼▼▼▼

FROM STANTON, MERCER COUNTY
North .5 mile on ND-37. The site's visitor center is east of the highway.
GPS 47.331417, -101.385636

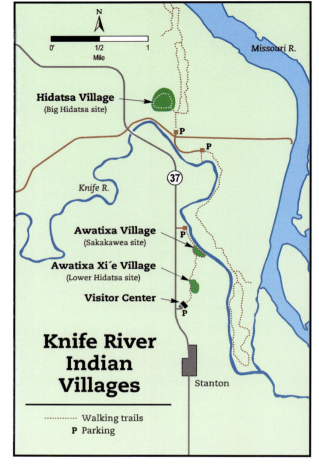

Reconstructed earthlodge near the visitor center.

Lake Jessie STATE HISTORIC SITE

LOCATED WEST of the town of Jessie, Griggs County, Lake Jessie State Historic Site marks the July 25 camp of the Nicollet-Frémont expedition of 1839. Joseph Nicolas Nicollet, a French astronomer and cartographer, came to the United States to study the physical geography of North America. He wanted to explore the region between the Mississippi and Missouri rivers in the area that now makes up the states of Minnesota, North Dakota, and South Dakota. Nicollet was assisted by John Charles Frémont, a lieutenant in the Topographical Bureau of the Corps of Engineers. The lake was named for Jessie Ann Benton, daughter of Senator Thomas Hart Benton of Missouri, who later married Frémont. Nicollet's 1843 "Hydrographic Basin" map, based on his expeditions, is a masterpiece of nineteenth-century cartography.

A campsite on the lake was also used by Isaac I. Stevens and his party on July 10–11, 1853, during a survey of a proposed railroad route. This was also a stopping point on July 15–16, 1862, on July 20, 1863, and in 1866 by James L. Fisk and his wagon trains on their way to the Montana gold fields (see **Fort Dilts**). Mail carriers who crossed through the area between 1867 and 1872 sought shelter on the east end of Lake Jessie.

Enclosed by a fence, the site is .29 acres of state land, located on top of a hill beside a farmyard. An aluminum cast marker on a fieldstone and concrete monument describe the events that took place there. A flagpole stands north of the marker.

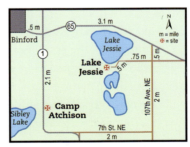

FROM BINFORD, GRIGGS COUNTY
East 3.6 miles on ND-65, south .5 mile on 107th Ave. NE, west .75 mile and southwest .5 mile on a dirt road past a farmhouse. The site is marked by an aluminum plaque on a small hill south of Lake Jessie.
GPS 47.540904, -98.290654

Lake Johnson STATE HISTORIC SITE

LAKE JOHNSON State Historic Site is named for Private George T. Johnson (a.k.a. Johnston), who drowned in the lake on August 11, 1865. Soldiers from the 3rd Illinois Cavalry Regiment, who were camping nearby, were enjoying a refreshing swim on a hot August day when Private Johnson accidently drowned. He was buried near the campsite, and a headstone and flagpole currently stand there in his memory. The site is located seven miles southwest of Cooperstown, Griggs County.

The 3rd Illinois Cavalry Regiment, commanded by Colonel Robert Huston Carnahan, was en route from Fort Abercrombie to Devils Lake. The regiment was assisting the 1865 reconnaissance expedition of General Alfred Sully, which was exploring the territory between Fort Rice and Devils Lake. The information gathered by the mission was used ultimately to select the location of Fort Totten (see **Fort Totten**).

This is not the only known historically significant event that transpired near Lake Johnson. The Nicollet-Frémont expedition in 1839 and the Isaac I. Stevens expedition in 1855 passed through this area (see **Lake Jessie**). On July 15, 1862, Captain James L. Fisk's wagon train of immigrants, who were traveling to the Montana gold fields, camped near the south end of this lake (see **Fort Dilts**). A year later on July 17, General Henry H. Sibley's military expedition crossed nearby heading toward Devils Lake (see **Sibley's and Sully's Northwest Indian Campaigns**). This area is also part of the ancestral homelands of the Dakotas.

During the late 1860s and 1870s, military and post roads connecting Fort Abercrombie, Fort Ransom, and Fort Totten ran within a half mile of this site. The trail junction lies about three miles to the south and slightly to the west.◄

FROM COOPERSTOWN, GRIGGS COUNTY

At the southeast corner of Cooperstown, south 6 miles on 114th Ave. NE and west 1 mile on Griggs Co. Rd. 22. The site is marked by a white marble headstone and flag pole north of the road.

GPS 47.355510, -98.135784

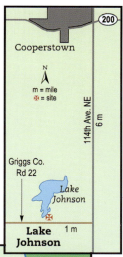

Forts Abercrombie, Ransom & Totten Military Trail

Maple Creek Crossing STATE HISTORIC SITE

MAPLE CREEK Crossing State Historic Site recognizes a stream crossing important to travel in the days before bridges. With its gently sloping banks and firm bottom, this ford across the Maple River was a landmark in the early days of the exploration and settlement of Dakota Territory. Located three miles south of Chaffee, Cass County, the .38 acre historic site lies immediately east of St. Peter's Lutheran Church on a grassy terrace near a bend in the river. The actual stream crossing is approximately one-half mile northwest of the site marker.

Euro-American use of the crossing may have occurred as early as 1822, when discouraged members of the Selkirk Colonies moved from the Pembina area to the Mississippi River near Fort Snelling (St. Paul, Minnesota). They followed an early fur trade trail along the western edge of the ancient Lake Agassiz shore line that crossed the Maple River.

By 1843 oxcart brigades of Norman Kittson and "Jolly" Joe Rolette were fording the Maple River on an established trade route between St. Paul and the Canadian border settlements of Pembina and St. Joseph (see **Walhalla**). Six years later, Major Samuel Woods led a military reconnaissance expedition across the ford.

General Isaac I. Stevens, recently appointed governor of the Washington Territory, crossed the river in 1853. His journey also included military exploration of the region to find a route for a transcontinental railroad. Nine years later, James L. Fisk led a party of immigrants across the ford en route to newly discovered gold fields in Montana.

In 1863 the Sibley expedition returned to Minnesota via the ford (see **Sibley's and**

Sully's Northwest Indian Campaigns). Camp Ambler, the Sibley army's bivouac on August 17, 1863, was located southeast of the Maple Creek marker. By the time the troops reached the stream, they were nearly exhausted. The expedition's surgeons reported that 433 men were affected by the summer heat. Of these, 150 were so sick they had to be transported by ambulance for at least part of the day's march. The men rested and recuperated at Camp Ambler until leaving early in the morning of August 19.

A sod structure, located a half mile to the southeast, served as a shelter for mail carriers, freighters, and others traveling the Fort Abercrombie-Fort Ransom-Fort Totten trails during the 1860s and 1870s. A wood-frame store and inn replaced the sod building, operated from 1879 until 1883 by James N. Watson.

The modern-day Maple Creek Crossing State Historic Site displays a marker on a masonry base made of stone from the first North Dakota Capitol, which burned on December 28, 1930. Although no visitor services are available and the ford is not visible from the site, the state property is accessible year-round. ◁

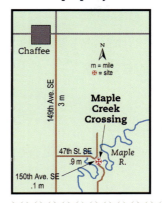

FROM CHAFFEE, CASS COUNTY
South 3 miles on 149th Ave. SE, east .9 mile on 47th St. SE, and southeast 0.1 mile on 150th Ave. SE. The site is marked by an aluminum plaque east across the road from a church.
GPS 46.728154, -97.325027

Photographed near the Canadian border, this Red River ox cart train probably used the Maple Creek crossing on its way to St. Paul, MN. SHSND A1934-1

Maple Creek Crossing ➤ 109

McPhail's Butte Overlook
STATE HISTORIC SITE

MCPHAIL'S BUTTE OVERLOOK State Historic Site marks one place from which Colonel Samuel McPhail directed movements of the 1st Minnesota Mounted Rangers during the Battle of Big Mound. For the full story of these events, see **Big Mound Battlefield**. This was the beginning of a weeklong series of battles, until the Sioux successfully escaped west of the Missouri River (see **Sibley's and Sully's Northwest Indian Campaigns**). The site is located seven-and-one-half miles north of Tappen, Kidder County.

Following the tragic opening of the battle, Colonel McPhail's cavalry prevented the Dakotas from escaping over the western edge of the plateau where they had been driven. As McPhail's troopers pursued people moving south off the plateau, a bolt of lightning struck, killing Private John Murphy and knocking two other soldiers to the ground.

McPhail's troops pursued the Dakotas for fourteen miles from the plateau to Dead Buffalo Lake, one mile north of the present-day town of Dawson. As darkness fell, the soldiers began setting up a temporary camp, but soon received orders to return to the main camp. The troops marched most of the night to return to Camp Sibley, gathering other regiments already encamped on the marshy plain.

A granite marker erected on top of a high hill denotes Colonel McPhail's vantage point overlooking the battle. There is, however, no access road, and a barbed wire fence separates the historic site from the county road. For access information, contact the Historic Preservation Division, State Historical Society of North Dakota, 612 East Boulevard Avenue, Bismarck, North Dakota, 58505, or call (701) 328-2666. ◄

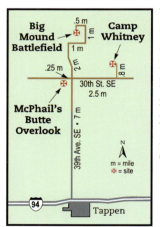

FROM TAPPEN, KIDDER COUNTY
North 7 miles on 39th Ave. SE and west .25 mile on 30th St. SE. The site is marked by a pink granite marker atop a hill south of the road.
GPS 46.980399,-99.641104

Medicine Rock STATE HISTORIC SITE

LOCATED ALONG the north fork of the Cannonball River, Medicine Rock State Historic Site is one of six known American Indian rock art sites in North Dakota. It is the largest of the rock art sites in the state and exhibits the greatest variety of pictures, called glyphs. Historically, the Mandan and Hidatsa Indians regarded Medicine Rock as an oracle, and it continues to be used by American Indians as a sacred site. Offerings of tobacco and cloth testify to the ongoing significance of this place as a religious shrine. Medicine Rock was a historic landmark well known to early European explorers.

The religious significance of the site was documented by Lewis and Clark in 1804, personnel of Stephen H. Long's expedition in 1819–1820, and German scientist and explorer Prince Alexander Philipp Maximilian in 1832–1834. It appears on historic maps from 1864 to 1872.

Although Meriwether Lewis and William Clark did not visit Medicine Rock, Clark's journal for February 21, 1805, states:

> The medicine-stone is the great oracle of the Mandans, and whatever it announces is believed with implicit confidence. Every spring, and on some occasions during the summer, a deputation visits the sacred spot, where there is a thick porous stone 20 feet in circumference, with a smooth surface. Having reached the place, the ceremony of smoking to it is performed by the deputies, who alternately take a whiff themselves and then present the pipe to the stone; after this they retire to an adjoining wood for the night, . . . in the morning they read the destinies of the nation in the white marks on the stone.[18]

Prince Maximilian reported in his journal of November 19, 1833: "A young Indian, Síh-Sä (Red Feather), spoke about the great medicine rock of which Lewis and Clark tell . . ." and "The Mandans, who call it the medicine boulder, Mih-Chöppenisch . . . and the Hidatsas, who know it by the name . . . Wihdä-Katachí . . . go there when their war parties move out."[19]

Incised or pecked pictures (petroglyphs) and painted figures (pictographs) cover the sandstone outcrop at Medicine Rock. Although eroded by time and, in some cases, defaced by vandals, many of the glyphs are identifiable. A rider on horseback, turtles, bighorn sheep, bear paw, handprint and footprint, bird track, and numerous hoof prints are visible.

Access to the site is difficult and crosses private land. For access information, contact the Historic Preservation Division, State Historical Society of North Dakota, 612 East Boulevard Avenue, Bismarck, North Dakota, 58505, or call (701) 328-2666. ◂

Close-up view of some of the petroglyphs sketched in group 9 of the overhead view.

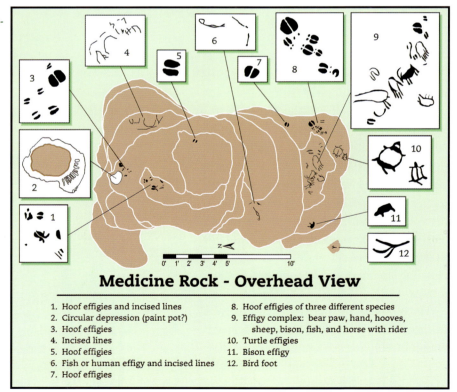

Medicine Rock - Overhead View

1. Hoof effigies and incised lines
2. Circular depression (paint pot?)
3. Hoof effigies
4. Incised lines
5. Hoof effigies
6. Fish or human effigy and incised lines
7. Hoof effigies
8. Hoof effigies of three different species
9. Effigy complex: bear paw, hand, hooves, sheep, bison, fish, and horse with rider
10. Turtle effigies
11. Bison effigy
12. Bird foot

Menoken Indian Village STATE HISTORIC SITE

MENOKEN INDIAN VILLAGE State Historic Site is located near the town of Menoken, east of Bismarck. This site marks the transition from a hunting and gathering way of life (Plains Woodland) to a culture of hunting and gardening maize, beans, sunflowers, and squash (Plains Village).

The community of about 200 people lived at the village from about AD 1200 to 1220. The village consisted of approximately thirty oval-shaped, earth-covered houses surrounded by a ditch and palisade, or wall made of wooden logs. Menoken Village was earlier than any settlement that can be linked with certainty to Mandan, Hidatsa, or Arikara peoples in North Dakota. However, the people who occupied Menoken Village were probably the ancestors of some of these historic village tribes.

The location was carefully chosen for its defensive features. The steep banks to the north and west would be difficult for intruders to climb. The rest of the village was protected by the palisade and the deep ditch, which encloses an area of almost one-and-one-half acres. The ditch formed a long arc, interrupted by four projecting loops, or bastions. The construction of the fortification system required organized labor and much timber.

The site was once thought to be the "Mantanne Fort" (Mandan village) visited by the 1738 La Vérendrye expedition. This was the assumption that led to the listing of the site as a National Historic Landmark in 1964. Later excavations revealed that the site is far older and is of national significance for different reasons. They indicate that the people living in Menoken were trading with horticultural villages farther south along the Missouri. The artifacts and architecture discovered at the site suggest that the change from gathering plants to gardening did not involve the migration of new people to the area. Rather, local cultural groups already living in the area were adopting new technologies and life ways.

Excavation of two houses in the village has revealed two styles of prehistoric architecture. One of the excavated houses was built in a pit about twenty inches below the ground surface, with only a few posts supporting ridge poles and walls of stacked sod. The other excavated house was built at surface level, with an earth-covered roof supported by many wall posts and support posts down the center of the house. The roofs of these houses were used for living and working areas, as was the case with later earthlodges.

The surface house also has a large bell-shaped storage pit behind it, similar to the kind used to store garden produce in later villages. This storage feature, along with the presence of some corncob fragments but no evidence of gardening tools, suggests that people were trading for corn but not growing any significant amounts themselves.

Stone, metal, and shell artifacts recovered at Menoken show that the people were involved in trade systems spanning the continent. Obsidian, whose nearest source is in what is now Yellowstone Park; raw copper, whose nearest source is in far-eastern Minnesota; and marine shells from the Atlantic or Gulf Coasts were all found here.

Although Menoken is not itself an early farming community, it has much to tell us about the origins of horticulture. It preserves that brief period in time when the moving frontier of a new way of life developed and expanded in this region.

A fieldstone kiosk at the entrance to the historic site contains a map and introduction to the village. Additional interpretive signs are located in the site. ◂

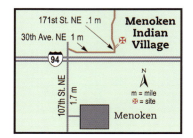

FROM MENOKEN, BURLEIGH COUNTY
North 1.7 miles on 107th St. NE, east 1 mile on 30th Ave. NE, and north 0.1 mile on 171st St. The dirt access road to the site is east of the road, and the site is marked by a fieldstone shelter.

GPS 46.841436, -100.518084

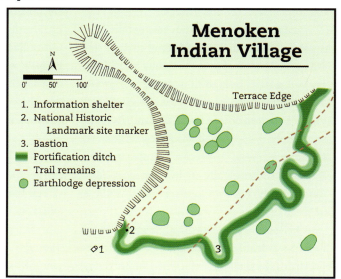

Molander Indian Village STATE HISTORIC SITE

MOLANDER INDIAN VILLAGE State Historic Site is a Hidatsa earthlodge village, located about twenty miles north of Mandan, in Oliver County, on the east side of Highway 1806. According to Lewis and Clark, the Awaxawi Hidatsa Indians lived in this village overlooking the Missouri River around 1764. Their neighbors, the Mandans, lived in similar villages centered around the mouth of the Heart River. The Awaxawi people are one of three groups of Hidatsas. Awaxawi (pronounced Ah-WAH-ha-WEE) means "Village on the Hill."

Hidatsa bands traditionally settled on the west side of the Missouri River in a region north of the Mandans. Hidatsa territory stretched from the hills called Square Buttes, south of the town of Price, Oliver County, to the mouth of the Yellowstone River. Molander Village is near the southern extent of this territory. The Awaxawi moved to this area from the east, arriving at Molander Village in the 1700s. They lived there until the 1781–1782 smallpox epidemic killed approximately one-half of their people. The survivors moved north to Amahami Village at the mouth of the Knife River. Today, a remnant of Amahami Village lies beside the Mercer County Courthouse in Stanton.

Faint depressions at Molander Village mark the locations of nearly forty houses, which were protected by a dry moat or fortification ditch. A wooden palisade stood on the inside edge of the ditch. There were six projections, called bastions, along the ditch. The bastions gave the villagers a clear view and open line of fire down the palisade walls. Each house, or earthlodge, measured forty to sixty feet in diameter and stood ten to fifteen feet high. An extended family of up to twenty people lived in each house.

Like the Mandans and Arikaras, Hidatsa Indians were farmers who grew crops in nearby gardens on the Missouri River floodplain. In 1968 test excavations at the site discovered seeds of flint corn (a hardy, early-ripening variety of maize), squash, beans, wild plum, wild grape, and wild cherry. Molander was a summer village occupied from spring through the fall. Each fall the inhabitants moved into temporary winter villages on the river bottoms where trees provided shelter and firewood.

There is a collapsed log cabin and stable near the eastern edge of the village. The buildings were reportedly built by an early settler around 1882 and are not related to the prehistoric site. The kiosk at the entrance to the village and the fieldstone markers were built by the Civilian Conservation Corps. Because Molander Village is surrounded by private land, please call the State Historical Society's Historic Preservation office at (701) 328-2666 for access information before attempting the trip. ◂

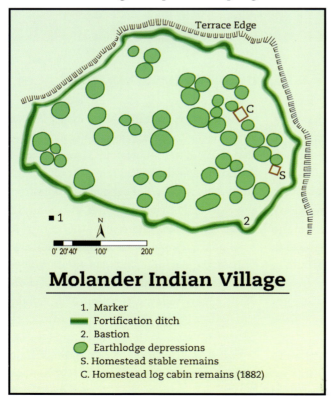

Molander Indian Village

1. Marker
— Fortification ditch
2. Bastion
● Earthlodge depressions
S. Homestead stable remains
C. Homestead log cabin remains (1882)

FROM PRICE, OLIVER COUNTY
North 3.1 miles on ND-1806. The site is marked by a kiosk east of the road.
GPS 47.124261, -100.966592

North Dakota Heritage Center and State Museum

THE EXPANDED Heritage Center is the headquarters of the State Historical Society of North Dakota and home to the State Museum. It is also home to the State Archives and the State Fossil Collection. The Heritage Center is on the state Capitol grounds in Bismarck, off Exit 159 on I-94. First opened in 1981, the 2014 expansion doubled the size of the Heritage Center.

Three museum galleries—the Adaptation Gallery: Geologic Time, the Innovation Gallery: Early Peoples and the Inspiration Gallery: Yesterday and Today—feature exhibits tracing North Dakota's history from 600 million years ago through the present day. The Treehouse, a children's exhibit, will introduce history through interactive play (opening 2015). The Governor's Gallery will host temporary and traveling exhibits and programs.

In the Geologic Time Gallery, exhibits discuss geology, environment, climate and life changes from millions of years ago through the last Ice Age in the state about 13,000 years ago. The exhibits feature impressive life size casts of animals such as *Tyrannosaurus rex* and saber-toothed cats, as well as hundreds of fossils of animals that once lived in North Dakota.

The Early Peoples Gallery is devoted to the earliest people of North Dakota. The story begins when people first migrated to North Dakota more than 13,000 years ago and continues up to the sovereign nations of today. Exhibits feature the museum's outstanding collection of quillwork, beadwork, baskets, and extensive archaeological artifacts. Historic murals were specially commissioned for this gallery to make the past vivid in the present.

The Yesterday and Today Gallery presents a look at the state and its people over the past

Northern Lights Atrium

Mastodon in Corridor of History

two centuries. It does so through six themes which unite us across time: Agricultural Innovation; Industry and Energy; Newcomers and Settlement; Conflict and War; Our Lives, Our Communities; and Cultural Expressions. Each area takes the visitor on a chronological exploration of that particular theme. Hundreds of artifacts from the museum's collections—from an original homestead shack to a 1960s fall-out shelter, a broken rifle and a baptismal gown—tell stories of how people were inspired by and adapted to changing times in North Dakota.

The Heritage Center houses extensive artifact, archaeological, paleontological, photographic, and archival collections. The State Archives in the Heritage Center is also open to the public. It acquires, preserves, and references all types of research material relating to North Dakota and the Northern Great Plains.

Its holdings include: manuscript collections, books, periodicals, maps, newspapers, audio, video, and digital materials, and photographs. The State Historic Preservation Office is also located in the Heritage Center.

The Museum Store has a unique selection of books, gifts, and handcrafted items. The James River Café offers light meals, snacks, and refreshments.

The North Dakota Heritage Center is open weekdays from 8 A.M. to 5 P.M.; Saturdays and Sundays from 10 A.M. to 5 P.M. Admission is free. The State Archives is open 8 A.M. to 4:30 P.M. weekdays and 10:30 A.M.–4:30 P.M. on the second Saturday of each month, except for legal holidays. SHSND offices are open from 8 A.M. to 5 P.M., Monday through Friday, except holidays. For more information call (701) 328-2666 or visit the website at history.nd.gov or statemuseum.nd.gov. ◄

Adaptation: Geologic Time Gallery

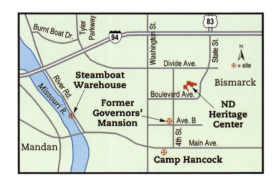

▼▼▼▼▼▼▼▼▼▼▼▼▼▼▼▼▼▼

AT BISMARCK, BURLEIGH COUNTY
State Capitol Grounds,
612 East Boulevard Ave.
GPS 46.819335, -100.778618

Innovation: Early Peoples Gallery

Heritage Center and State Museum

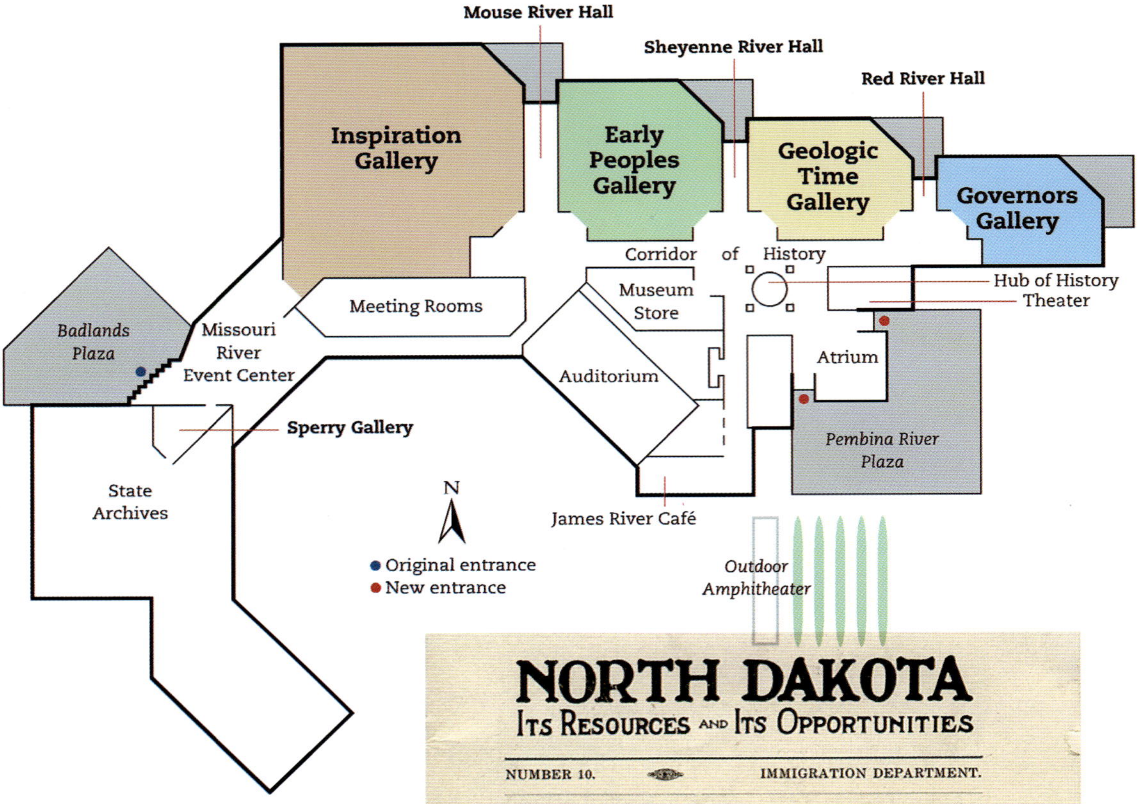

Mouse River Hall

Sheyenne River Hall

Red River Hall

Inspiration Gallery

Early Peoples Gallery

Geologic Time Gallery

Governors Gallery

Corridor of History

Hub of History Theater

Meeting Rooms

Museum Store

Badlands Plaza

Missouri River Event Center

Auditorium

Atrium

Sperry Gallery

Pembina River Plaza

State Archives

N

James River Café

● Original entrance
● New entrance

Outdoor Amphitheater

Among the themes of the Yesterday and Today Gallery is Newcomers and Settlement. Included in the exhibit is this 1920 publication from the North Dakota Immigration Department, touting the sunshine state's advantages. SHSND F631.N67

NORTH DAKOTA
ITS RESOURCES AND ITS OPPORTUNITIES

NUMBER 10.   IMMIGRATION DEPARTMENT.

MORE DAYS OF SUNSHINE THAN ANY STATE IN U.S.

BETTER GRAIN GRADES.
PAY FOR DOCKAGE
BETTER MARKETING FACILITIES
COÖPERATIVE PACKING PLANT
STATE ELEVATOR AND FLOUR MILL
UNDER CONSTRUCTION
THE STATE OF THE HOME-OWNER ~
MORE DEMOCRACY THAN IN ANY
OTHER STATE IN THE UNION
(THE INITIATIVE AND REFERENDUM)
OPPORTUNITY AND PROSPERITY
FOR ALL

THE SUNSHINE STATE
BIDS YOU WELCOME

North Dakota Lewis and Clark Interpretive Center and Fort Mandan

LOCATED AT THE intersection of US Highway 83 and North Dakota Highway 200A at Washburn, the Lewis and Clark Interpretive Center provides an overview of the Lewis and Clark Expedition, with special emphasis on the time the expedition spent at Fort Mandan during the winter of 1804–05. It features state-of-the-art interactive exhibits and rare Lewis & Clark era artifacts—including one of only six working air rifles in the world—as well as world-famous art collections. In September 2013, the center expanded to include a 180-seat event center, research library, and additional meeting room space available to rent.

The Fort Clark exhibit in the Interpretive Center tells the story of the Mandan and Arikara village and fur trade posts located at **Fort Clark Trading Post**, fifteen miles away off Highway 200A. Built as a fur trading post for the American Fur Company, Fort Clark became a cultural crossroads. Visitors to the site during the 1830s included Prince Maximilian of Wied and the Swiss artist, Karl Bodmer. The Interpretive Center is one of four galleries in the world to house a complete collection of Karl Bodmer prints. Bodmer's aquatints and Maximilian's written descriptions are considered among the most complete and reliable eyewitness accounts of the upper Midwest

Indian cultures. The "Our Agrarian Heritage" exhibit features the story of agriculture in North Dakota beginning with Our First Farmers and leading up to present-day agriculture. The exhibit also includes a Centennial Farms interactive kiosk.

A full-sized reconstruction of Fort Mandan, the home of the Lewis and Clark Expedition during the winter of 1804–05, stands along the Missouri River less than two miles from the center. It is not certain how close this site is to the original Fort Mandan, which burned during the winter following the expedition's stay. Most scholars believe that the site of the original fort has been flooded by the Missouri River.

The reconstruction of the fort, completed forty years ago, was based upon descriptions found in the journals of the expedition. Patrick Gass, a member of the expedition, described the fort as follows:

The Fort Clark exhibit in the interpretive center shows the trade goods that would have been present at Fort Clark during the fur trade era.

[T]he huts were in two rows, containing four rooms each, and joined at one end forming an angle. When raised about seven feet high a floor of puncheons or split plank were laid, and covered with grass and clay; which made a warm loft. The upper part projected a foot over and the roofs were made shed-fashion, rising from the inner side, and making the outer wall about eighteen feet high. The part not enclosed by the huts we intended to picket. In the angle formed by the two rows of huts we built two rooms, for holding our provisions and stores.[20]

The fort was constructed of the cottonwood timber found along the Missouri. Construction began on November 3, 1804, and Gass records that by the evening of November 27, they had completed the roofs of their huts, which were made of "puncheon split out of cotton wood and then hewed." That night, seven inches of snow fell, and the following day was stormy.

A steady stream of Mandan and Hidatsa Indians visited during the five months the expedition spent at Fort Mandan, trading goods and information about the land to the west. Lewis and Clark and other members of the expedition also made frequent visits to the nearby villages and went on joint hunting trips with the villagers during that winter. On April 7, 1805, the expedition left Fort Mandan, on their way to the Pacific Ocean, after spending longer at this location than they would anywhere else on their journey.

The Fort Mandan replica site features the Headwaters Fort Mandan Visitor Center constructed of coal combustion products, walking trails along the Missouri, children's playground, Fahlgren Park with picnic shelters and other conveniences. The fort is located on

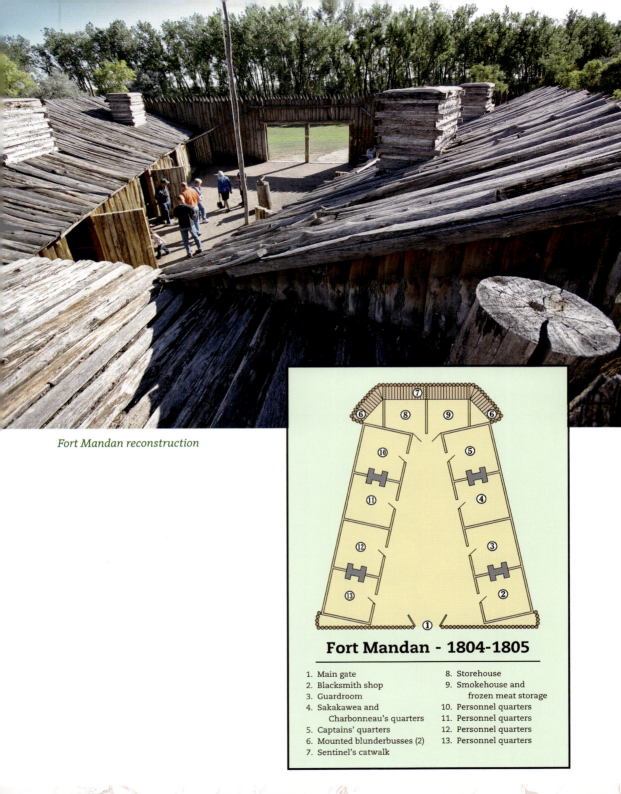

Fort Mandan reconstruction

Fort Mandan - 1804-1805

1. Main gate
2. Blacksmith shop
3. Guardroom
4. Sakakawea and Charbonneau's quarters
5. Captains' quarters
6. Mounted blunderbusses (2)
7. Sentinel's catwalk
8. Storehouse
9. Smokehouse and frozen meat storage
10. Personnel quarters
11. Personnel quarters
12. Personnel quarters
13. Personnel quarters

Lewis & Clark Interpretive Center and Fort Mandan   www.history.nd.gov

McLean County Highway 17, two miles west of the Lewis & Clark Interpretive Center at Washburn, near the intersection of US Highway 83 and ND Highway 200A.

The Interpretive Center and Fort Mandan are operated by the Lewis and Clark Fort Mandan Foundation and are open year-round. Both sites are open daily from 9 A.M. to 5 P.M., Monday-Saturday and noon–5 P.M. Sundays. Memorial Day-Labor Day open 9 A.M.–5 P.M. every day. The admission fee is $7.50 for adults, $5.00 for students, and members are free (includes admission to both sites). Special rates are available for pre-scheduled school and group tours. For more information, contact the Lewis & Clark Fort Mandan Foundation, P.O. Box 607, Washburn, ND 58577-0607, call (701) 462-8535 or toll-free (877) 462-8535, or visit www.FortMandan.com. ◂

▾▾▾▾▾▾▾▾▾▾▾▾▾▾▾▾▾▾

FROM JUNCTION US-83 AND ND-200A AT WASHBURN, McLEAN COUNTY

South 0.1 mile on ND-200A, and west 0.1 mile on 8th St. SW. The interpretive center is on the south side of the road. For the Fort Mandan reconstruction, travel west a further 2 miles on 8th St. SW and south .3 mile. The site is east of the road.
GPS 47.301257, -101.041635

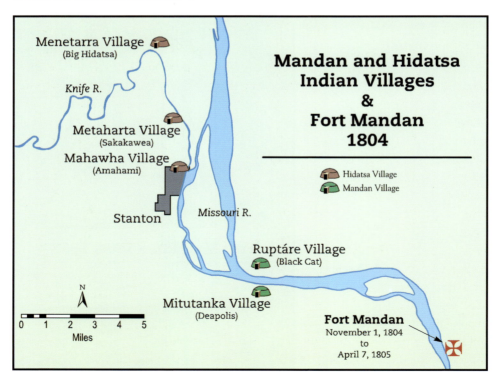

Oak Lawn Church STATE HISTORIC SITE

AT THE JUNCTION of Highway 5 and Highway 32 in Pembina County, a peaceful cemetery rests in a grove of trees. Beside it, a fieldstone marker describes the log Presbyterian church that once stood near the cemetery, Oak Lawn Church.

The Reverend Ransom Waite, a Presbyterian minister from Mankato, Minnesota, settled in Beaulieu Township in 1883 to serve the surrounding communities. Two years later, the local congregation built a log church. Although the building lacked a floor when the first services were held, Waite and the trustees were soon able to secure a $300 loan from the home missions to install a permanent roof and floor. Planks served as seats until chairs and a pulpit were purchased a short time later.

To expand the use of the church, the congregation passed a resolution to allow any Protestant denomination to worship in the building, and as a result, Baptists and Methodists also held services there. Sometime prior to 1910, services were discontinued, but the local community continued to maintain the building and cemetery. The property was deeded to the State Historical Society of North Dakota on November 18, 1933. A grass fire destroyed the church on November 6, 1954.

FROM CONCRETE, PEMBINA COUNTY
North 1 mile on 127th Ave. NE, southwest of the junction of ND-32 and ND-5. The site is marked by an aluminum plaque west of the road.
GPS 48.760557, -97.927918

Palmer's Spring STATE HISTORIC SITE

PALMER'S SPRING State Historic Site, near Esmond, Benson County, overlooks the location where on August 23, 1868, six soldiers from the 31st Infantry and two civilian scouts escorting a mail wagon stopped for their midday rest and were attacked by Yankton and Blackfeet Indians. The Indians launched their attack from behind a large, limestone boulder (visible above), and three of the soldiers were killed in the first two volleys. Two other soldiers escaped to a bank near the spring, and a civilian scout survived by hiding behind a wagon wheel. Another civilian scout (Frank Palmer, below) and a soldier teamster had taken a horse to the spring for water and escaped the initial attack.

When Palmer and the teamster heard the commotion, they ran to the bluff above the spring and fired at the Indians. The Indians were riding off on the soldiers' mules when the two soldiers, hidden in the spring bank recovered their weapons and fired at them. After the Indians withdrew, Palmer rode the one remaining horse to Fort Totten to get help. The surviving soldiers hid the mail and surplus arms and followed on foot. A relief party was dispatched from Fort Totten on August 24, 1868, recovering the wagon, mail, and supplies. The bodies of the dead were also taken back to Fort Totten for burial.

Palmer's Spring shows little change after the passage of almost a century and a half. The limestone boulder stands at its original location. Frank Palmer, for whom the spring was named, spent the remainder of his life in the Fort Totten-Crary area and served as a delegate to the original North Dakota Constitutional Convention in 1889.

SHSND A3112

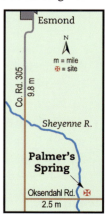

FROM ESMOND, BENSON COUNTY

South 9.8 miles on County Road 305, and east 2.5 miles on Oksendahl Road. The site is unmarked on the north side of the road. **GPS** 47.890746, -99.719081

Pembina State Museum

SITUATED AT THE border of Minnesota, North Dakota, and Manitoba, the Pembina State Museum, located off Exit 215 on I-29 in Pembina, tells the story of a region that has been a center of activity for centuries. The Pembina area was home to several groups of native peoples, including the Ojibwas, Dakotas, Assiniboines, and Crees. With their families, they lived, hunted buffalo, and gathered wild berries here.

The region also played an important role in the fur trade business. From this trade a new nation of people were born, the Métis, who were descendants of European traders and Indian women. Early fur trade posts and colonies led to the establishment of a river town named Pembina. The scene of international politics and major transportation routes, the region has served as a gateway of commerce between Canada and the United States since the early 1800s.

The museum features a permanent exhibit gallery that presents 100 million years of the region's history, starting with fossils from a Cretaceous sea, to glacial Lake Agassiz, and extending to the present day. Visitors can learn about the diverse peoples who call Pembina home, including native Indian peoples and Euro-American settlers. Exhibits include stone and bone tools of the first peoples, a Red River oxcart, and other objects related to Pembina's fur trade industry. Other exhibits continue the story of the frontier military forts and the US and Canadian border survey. The visitor can also explore the story of Euro-American agricultural settlement, including objects from Ukrainian and Icelandic settlers, and the transportation networks that continue to play a role in the economics of the region. A temporary gallery features unique exhibits from contemporary art to artifact-rich history.

The observation tower of the museum offers a stunning view of the Red River Valley from seven stories above the ground. On a clear day visitors have a 360-degree view for ten miles: a neatly organized patchwork of modern farmlands and evidence of the region's historic sites, industry, transportation, and communications. A travel information center contains information about other sites of interest in North Dakota. The museum store offers a unique selection of books and items, many crafted by North Dakotans, that reflect and enhance the museum exhibit themes.

The Pembina State Museum is open year-round. From May 16 to September 15, the hours are 9 A.M. to 6 P.M., Monday through Saturday and from 1 to 6 P.M. on Sunday. From September 16 to May 15 the museum closes at 5 P.M. every day. The museum is ADA accessible.

Admission is free for the exhibits and museum store, but there is an admission fee for the observation tower. For more information, contact the Pembina State Museum, P.O. Box 456, Pembina ND 58271 or (701) 825-6840. ◄

AT PEMBINA, PEMBINA COUNTY
From the I-29 exit #215, east off-ramp, north 0.1 mile.
GPS 48.973235, -97.254243

Pembina politician and fur trader Joseph Rolette created a trail between Pembina and St. Paul, Minnesota, using Red River ox carts to divert a substantial part of trade away from the rival Hudson's Bay Company in Canada. Rolette served six terms in the Minnesota Territorial Legislature. He served as Pembina postmaster and US customs officer until his death in Pembina in 1871. Minnesota Historical Society image

Pembina State Museum

Pulver Mounds STATE HISTORIC SITE

PULVER MOUNDS State Historic Site preserves two low, conical burial mounds on a small bluff above Coal Lake, southeast of Underwood, McLean County. Burial mounds such as these were typically constructed during the Woodland period from approximately 100 B.C. to A.D. 600 (see **Standing Rock**). At that time Woodland peoples buried their dead in a carefully prepared subterranean burial chamber, and then marked the cemetery with a round pile of earth over the grave, called a conical mound. Mound sites are complex grave sites often used for hundreds of years; some are known to have been used for more than 1,000 years. Later, Plains Village groups sometimes used the tops of existing burial mounds as places of interment.

Conical mounds in North Dakota generally range in height from two to twenty-five feet, and in diameter from ten to sixty feet. The two mounds at the Pulver Mounds site are approximately forty-five feet in diameter and are three to five feet high. These burial grounds or cemeteries are sacred to many American Indians. In the state of North Dakota, mounds are classified as unmarked burial sites and are protected by law from disturbance.

The Falkirk Mining Company donated this significant prehistoric burial site to the State of North Dakota with the State Historical Society acting as trustee. Access to the site is difficult and there are no interpretive materials at the site. For access information, contact the Historic Preservation Division, State Historical Society of North Dakota, 612 East Boulevard Avenue, Bismarck, North Dakota, 58505, or call (701) 328-2666. ◂

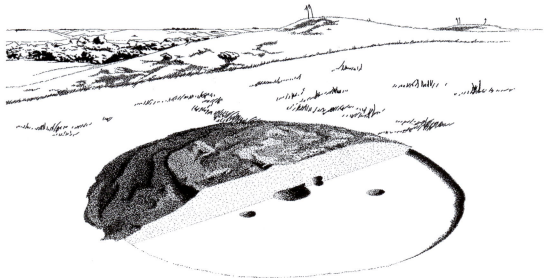

As shown in the illustration, burial mounds were often located on the crest of a hill overlooking a lake or river valley. The contour map on the right shows that the placement of Pulver Mounds follows the traditional methods. The cross-section, above, shows one stage of construction and related burial features in a burial mound. The dark, circular depressions are graves.

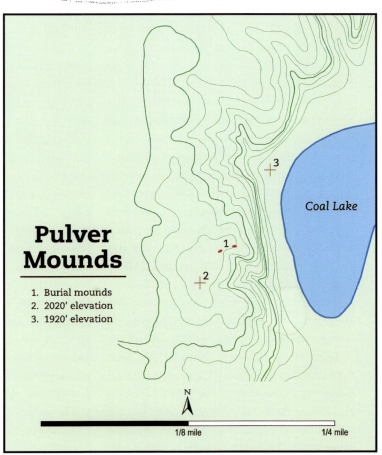

Pulver Mounds

1. Burial mounds
2. 2020' elevation
3. 1920' elevation

Ronald Reagan Minuteman Missile
STATE HISTORIC SITE

THE RONALD REAGAN Minuteman Missile State Historic Site near Cooperstown served an important role as part of the United States' strategy of nuclear deterrence during the Cold War years. The post-World War II confrontation between the United States and the Union of Soviet Socialist Republics (USSR) put our military on continuous alert in a massive arms race, although the two superpowers never fought each other directly. The US Air Force started deploying solid-fuel Minuteman missiles near bases in Montana, Missouri, Wyoming, and the Dakotas in the 1960s.

Directly on the front lines of the Cold War, the Ronald Reagan Minuteman Missile State Historic Site preserves and interprets the story of the Minuteman missile system as well as the people working in and living around the missile sites. Constructed as part of the Grand Forks Air Force Base's 321 Strategic Missile Wing, the Oscar-Zero Missile Alert Facility (MAF) and the November-33 Launch Facility (LF) became fully operational with installed Minuteman II missiles in 1966. A map showing the location of the missile wing launch facilities is provided on page 188.

The Oscar-Zero MAF consists of an aboveground Launch Control Support Building (LCSB) that housed eight enlisted personnel who provided security, maintenance, and support. The LCSB also provided access to the underground Launch Control Center (LCC). Each LCC housed a two-officer crew that was responsible for monitoring, launching, and retargeting its flight of ten nuclear missiles. Each LCC was linked by means of underground cables and a radio network to ten missile silos (or LFs) in its flight and other LCCs in its squadron.

Missileers worked twenty-four-hour shifts, called "alerts" every three days, averaging eight alerts per month. Two-member crews monitored the missiles and awaited orders twenty-four hours a day, seven days a week, 365 days a year.

Support personnel remained topside, in the LCSB. Two three-person security teams were on duty day and night. A flight security controller coordinated response to alarms at the remote LFs as well as controlling the security of, and permitting access to, the MAFs. Along with these security forces, there was also a facility manager on site, responsible for the care of the entire MAF. A chef singlehandedly fed hungry team members several times a day as well as visitors such as the large maintenance teams or high-ranking officers.

Many maintenance teams serviced the sites. Electro-mechanical teams, missile maintenance teams, missile handling teams, communication teams, civilian contractors and many other teams regularly moved throughout the missile sites.

The blast-hardened complex approximately fifty feet below the building consists of both the LCC and a Launch Control Equipment Building (LCEB). The underground steel-reinforced concrete LCC contains equipment for monitoring and launching the ten missiles. It also contains life support equipment and minimal accommodations for two duty officers. The LCEB provides environmental control and power to the LCC. The LCC and LCEB are protected by massive blast doors and were designed to be self-sufficient over prolonged periods, such as during a nuclear attack.

November-33 LF was a self-contained underground concrete-lined steel missile silo with blast doors, an associated Launcher Equipment Room, and an adjacent underground Launcher Equipment Building. The LF was decommissioned, the missile was removed, and the silo was filled in as a result of the Strategic Arms Reduction Treaty (START) of 1991. Today, the site includes the above-ground concrete blast door that originally covered the missile in its silo. In the event of a launch, the door would be blown off the silo by sliding horizontally along rails, which are still in place. The access hatch for crews to service the missile is still there, and the whole site is surrounded by the original eight-foot security fence. The electronic surveillance system is also still in place.

Oscar Zero consists of the above-ground support building (opposite page) and the underground Launch Control Center, which houses the command chair for the launching of nuclear missiles.

For nearly thirty years these two missile facilities were on continuous alert. While the Cold War did not escalate into a full-scale shooting war, the US continued to develop and stockpile increasingly sophisticated weapons. The single-warhead Minuteman II missile at November-33 LF and those controlled by Oscar-Zero MAF were replaced in the early 1970s by the new Minuteman III, which had greater range and could deliver three warheads to widely scattered targets.

Following a dramatic arms race in the 1980s, the Cold War showed signs of ending with the fall of the Berlin Wall and the collapse of Soviet-Bloc countries in Eastern Europe. START, signed by the United States and the Soviet Union in 1991, occurred just before the collapse of the USSR. START limited the number of strategic weapons on both sides, eventually resulting in the closing of the 321 Wing at Grand Forks AFB and the removal of all Minuteman missiles from the base. Each LF and MAF was dynamited or filled, except Oscar-Zero MAF, which was preserved by the US Air Force to become a state historic site in 2007. It is now on the National Register of Historic Places.

A Minuteman III missile field with 150 nuclear-tipped Minuteman missiles is still operating in North Dakota, based out of Minot Air Force Base.

The Ronald Reagan Minuteman Missile State Historic Site is open to the public from March 16 to October 31. Between May 16 and September 15 the site is open daily. Tours of the site can be obtained by appointment between November 1 and the last day of February. There is an admission fee for tours of Oscar-Zero MAF. State Historical Society of North Dakota Foundation members and children aged five and under are admitted free; school groups pay reduced admission. Oscar-Zero is located four miles north of Cooperstown on Highway 45, and November-33 is two miles east of Cooperstown on Highway 200. Brochures describing each are available at the site or from the State Historical Society of North Dakota. For more information, contact the site supervisor, Ronald Reagan Minuteman Missile State Historic Site, 555 113th ½ Avenue NE Hwy 45, Cooperstown, North Dakota, 58425, or call (701) 797-3691. ◂

November 33 still has the above-ground concrete blast door that originally covered the missile. The missile silo complex, now filled in, is shown on the diagram.

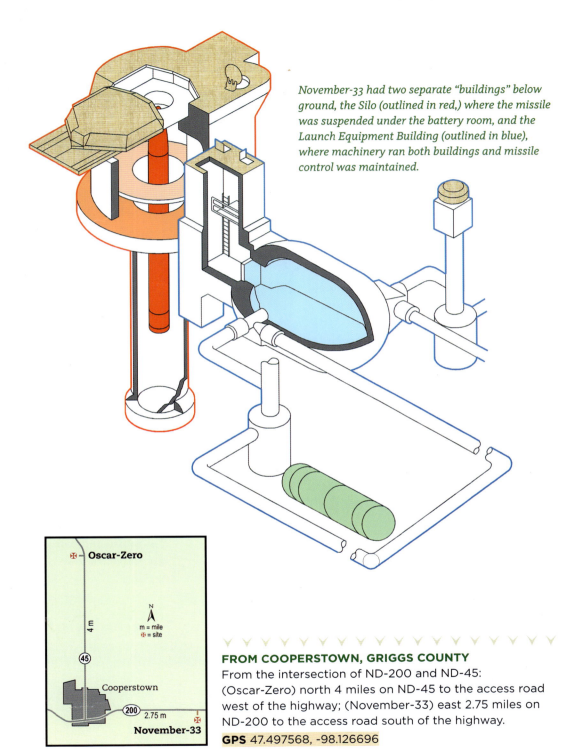

November-33 had two separate "buildings" below ground, the Silo (outlined in red,) where the missile was suspended under the battery room, and the Launch Equipment Building (outlined in blue), where machinery ran both buildings and missile control was maintained.

FROM COOPERSTOWN, GRIGGS COUNTY
From the intersection of ND-200 and ND-45: (Oscar-Zero) north 4 miles on ND-45 to the access road west of the highway; (November-33) east 2.75 miles on ND-200 to the access road south of the highway.
GPS 47.497568, -98.126696

St. Claude
STATE HISTORIC SITE

THE ST. CLAUDE State Historic Site was deeded to the State of North Dakota in 1927 as a memorial to Father John Malo. It is located about two miles northwest of present-day St. John, Rolette County. The site contains the archaeological remains of an 1882 mission and its cemetery. A stone marker on the site bears the inscription: "The Old Mission, St. Claude, May 3, 1882 by Pere J. F. Malo." A larger wooden sign describes some of the history of the site, and depressions mark several of the forty-seven graves recorded in the parish cemetery registry.

Father John Malo (inset, above, SHSND A6568), a missionary priest, came to the Turtle Mountains in 1881 with settlers from Quebec, Canada, to found a mission. He built a small log building, twenty feet by forty feet, with living quarters in the attic and a chapel on the main floor. Father Malo christened the mission St. Claude and opened the church on May 3, 1882. Later, the parish grew as Métis families moved in from the Red River settlements in Manitoba, and an addition, equal in size to the original building, was built onto the chapel.

When the St. Paul, Minneapolis, and Manitoba Railroad reached the area in the mid-1880s, it was decided that the church should be relocated closer to the railroad line. The St. Claude mission buildings were abandoned, and a new wood-frame church, St. John the Baptist, was built in 1887, two miles from St. Claude. This new church became the nucleus of the town of St. John.

FROM ST. JOHN, ROLETTE COUNTY
North .25 mile on Foussard Ave., west .25 mile on ND-43, and north 1.25 miles on 45thAve. NE. The site is east of the road and marked by a carved granite stone and a sign .25 mile east along a dirt road.
GPS 48.968729, -99.721793

Sitting Bull Burial

AT THE WEST EDGE of the town of Fort Yates, Standing Rock Sioux Reservation, Sioux County, is a monument to the great Hunkpapa Lakota leader, Tȟatȟáŋka Íyotake, or Sitting Bull. The monument marks his original grave, and was a state historic site until it was returned to the management of the Standing Rock Sioux Tribe in 2007. Sitting Bull was an inspired leader of his people during a extremely difficult era of conflict between the American military and the native peoples of the Northern Plains. His grand-niece, the founding president of Sitting Bull College, describes him as follows:

> He was the prophet or the spiritual man, the spiritual leader.... He's the one that goes up to the high mountains and prays.
>
> *Zona Loans Arrow*

Sitting Bull was born near the Grand River in what is now South Dakota in the early 1830s. While still a young man, he demonstrated his intelligence, courage, and leadership. The Strong Heart Society (a warrior society) and the Hunkpapas recognized him as a war chief in 1857. In the 1860s he led forces from several tribes resisting Euro-American intrusion and during the 1870s he was a regional leader fighting the United States Army.

In 1876 the army ordered free-roving bands of Indians confined to the reservations created in southern Dakota Territory. Lieutenant George Armstrong Custer and the 7th Cavalry left Fort Abraham Lincoln, south of Bismarck, in pursuit of a large band of Native Americans hunting in what is now Montana. They attacked a large encampment of Hunkpapas, Brulés, Sans Arcs, Miniconjous, Oglalas, Sihasapa Lakotas, and Cheyennes camped near the Little Bighorn River. Sitting Bull was not the military leader in the battle that followed. He was, however, a political and spiritual leader of his people, who decisively defeated Custer and his forces.

The War and Interior Departments pursued the victorious Indian people, including Sitting Bull and his followers, who retreated across the border into Canada. By July 1881 the bison had almost completely disappeared and food was scarce. Sitting Bull and thirty-five families returned to Fort Buford where he gave his weapons to his son to surrender to the fort's commander, Major D. H. Brotherton. (see **Fort Buford**).

Sitting Bull was sent to a military prison at Fort Randall for two years before moving to Standing Rock. In 1884 he accepted a number of offers to appear before the non-Indian public. People were fascinated by the leader said to have stopped the United States Army and won the most famous battle of the Indian wars. A notable event was his tour with Buffalo Bill Cody's Wild West Show.

Sitting Bull argued against and refused to sign the Great Sioux Agreement of 1889, which greatly reduced the size of the South Dakota Sioux reservations, allocated land to individuals, and opened land to homesteaders. The government managed to pressure enough people into signing, but Sitting Bull's continuing opposition made it more difficult for the Indian agents. Shortly after, the Ghost Dance spread to the Northern Plains. This religious movement centered around the doctrines of a Paiute holy man named Wovoka, who believed that by dancing a special dance, Indians could enter a peaceful, rich land free of white men. Furthermore, a special garment (a Ghost Dance shirt) protected the wearer from bullets. In 1890 some of Sitting Bull's followers participated in the movement at Standing Rock, and Sitting Bull observed some of the Ghost Dance ceremonies.

When rumors began to spread among white settlers that the Ghost Dance would spark a Sioux uprising, the Indian Police were sent to arrest him. On December 15, 1890, as he was taken from his cabin, a number of his supporters resisted, and a fight broke out. Sitting Bull, seven of his followers, and six Indian Police died in the ensuing struggle.

On December 17, 1890, army officers and

Sitting Bull, 1884. SHSND A2250-0001

Wearing a Strong Heart Society war bonnet, Sitting Bull uses his lance to count coup on a Crow warrior. Image drawn by his cousin No Two Horns. SHSND 9380.41

the Indian Agent James McLaughlin buried Sitting Bull without ceremony in a military cemetery at Fort Yates. Some of Sitting Bull's people fled to Pine Ridge Reservation, where many died in the massacre at Wounded Knee on December 29, 1890. This massacre signaled the tragic end to the epic struggle between the Sioux and the United States Army that began with the US-Dakota War of 1862 (see **Sibley's and Sully's Northwest Indian Campaigns**).

Many years after his unceremonious burial, the son of Sitting Bull's brother-in-law, Waŋblí Ȟóta (Clarence Gray Eagle), requested that the Lakota leader's remains be moved to Grand River, South Dakota. The request was denied by the state of North Dakota. Under the cover of darkness in April 1953, Gray Eagle led an expedition to move Sitting Bull's body. The expedition dug into the site and removed bones, which they believed to be those of the great leader, and reburied them near Mobridge. Today, monuments stand in Sitting Bull's honor at both locations.

AT FORT YATES, SIOUX COUNTY

The site is located on the west edge of Fort Yates on the north side of 92nd St. and is marked by an aluminum plaque.

GPS 46.088725, -100.633771

Standing Rock STATE HISTORIC SITE

PERCHED ON A HIGH HILL overlooking the Sheyenne River in Ransom County are a series of four interconnected burial mounds. Three of the mounds are circular, artificial hills in the shape of low cones. The fourth is a linear mound, which extends in a straight line. It begins west of the central mounds and runs east to the farthest conical mound (see map). The site is named after a large boulder that stands on the top of the largest mound.

Burial mounds are human cemeteries that contain multiple graves and were built primarily during the middle of the Woodland period, dating from 100 B.C. to A.D. 600 (see **Pulver Mounds**). Some mounds continued to be used as a place of interment for more than a thousand years. A single conical mound can contain up to thirty-five individuals.

Travelers used the Standing Rock mounds as a Sheyenne Valley landmark. The 1843 "Hydrographical Basin" map prepared by Joseph Nicollet identifies "Inyan Bosndata or Standing Rock" (see trails map on page 184). The correct spelling should be *Inyán Bosdáta*, which means "Standing Rock" in Dakota. Nicollet and John C. Frémont camped within sight of the site on Monday, August 12, 1839 (see **Lake Jessie** for more information about the Nicollet and Frémont expedition). From March 1881 to July 1884, the local post office was called "Standingrock," because the Post Office Department refused to accept post office names of more than one word.

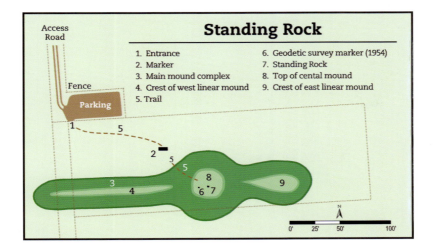

The site is two miles east of Little Yellowstone Park, near Enderlin, Ransom County. The access road to the site climbs a steep hill and access depends on weather and road conditions. There is a gravel parking lot at the top of the hill. A monument beside the mounds gives a brief description of the significance of this prehistoric cemetery. ◄

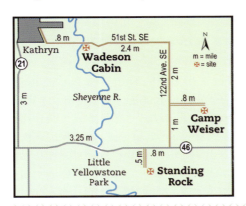

FROM KATHRYN, BARNES COUNTY
South 3 miles on ND-21, east 3.25 miles on ND-46, and south .5 mile on a steep dirt road to the site's parking area. The site is marked by three mounds, a large cylindrical stone, and an aluminum plaque south of the road.

GPS 46.623505, -97.908611

The large boulder that stands atop the largest mound has given the site its name.

Steamboat Warehouse STATE HISTORIC SITE

THE STEAMBOAT WAREHOUSE Historic Marker, located on the east bank of the Missouri River in Bismarck across the road from the water treatment plant on River Road (Highway 1804), commemorates the Northern Pacific Railroad warehouse built to store goods in transshipment between steamboats and freight trains. The 300-foot-long stone and frame warehouse was constructed in 1883 and was torn down in 1925. The interpretive marker also describes activity at the dock adjacent to the warehouse.

From 1872 to 1887 Bismarck was an important transportation center and Missouri River port. Freight was hauled to Bismarck from the East by the Northern Pacific Railroad. Until a railroad bridge across the Missouri was completed October 21, 1882, the railroad terminated at the east side of the river and resumed on the west side. During the winter, trains crossed the ice on specially built track and during the summer, they were ferried across. A line called the River Landing Spur ran down to the steamboat warehouse so that freight from the railroad could be transferred to steamboats for shipping via the Missouri River. The river connected St. Louis, Missouri, Fort Benton, Montana, and ports in between.

The dock area included other warehouses,

saloons, hotels, restaurants, and gambling establishments built to service the transient river trade. Bismarck was a major distribution point and travel center during that time and continued to serve in a reduced manner even after the railroad continued west in 1883.

This 3.21 acre site displays a fieldstone monument with an aluminum plaque and is open year-round. A small parking area is in front of the marker on the west side of the road. ◀

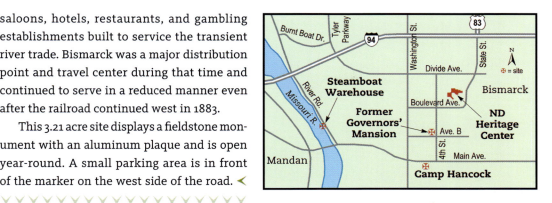

FROM I-94 EXIT #157 AT BISMARCK, BURLEIGH COUNTY
North 0.1 mile on Tyler Parkway, west .8 mile on Burnt Boat Road, and south 1.4 miles. The site is marked by an aluminum plaque west of the road.
GPS 46.814582, -100.821417

ABOVE. The interior of the warehouse in 1902.
SHSND 00124-0003

LEFT. A steamboat, the warehouse, and in the distance, the brewery in Bismarck, 1886.
SHSND E0155

Stutsman County Courthouse
STATE HISTORIC SITE

STUTSMAN COUNTY Courthouse, located at 504 Third Avenue SE in Jamestown, is the oldest surviving courthouse in North Dakota and is listed on the National Register of Historic Places. During the days of the Dakota Territory, meetings were held in the courthouse in preparation for statehood. The building is considered a superb but rare example in the Upper Midwest of the Gothic-Revival style of architecture. The interior is outstanding for its stamped metal ornamentation that dates to 1905.

Designed by Henry C. Koch, a Wisconsin architect who worked as General Philip H. Sheridan's topographic engineer during the Civil War, the courthouse construction was completed in 1883. An addition designed by Gilbert R. Horton, a Jamestown architect, was added on the rear of the courthouse in 1926 to handle the growing needs of Stutsman County. The building served as the center of county government until the early 1980s when a new courthouse was built, adjoining and incorporating the earlier addition.

Restoration efforts have stabilized the exterior of the courthouse. Rehabilitation of the interior initially focused on structural and mechanical repairs and is ongoing. To make a contribution to the restoration of this significant monument, contact the State Historical Society of North Dakota, 612 E. Boulevard Ave., Bismarck, North Dakota, 58205, or call (701) 328-2666.

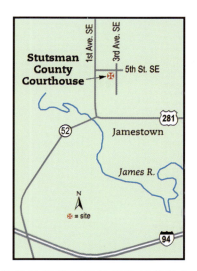

AT JAMESTOWN, STUTSMAN COUNTY
504 3rd Ave. SE, at the intersection with 5th St. SE.
GPS 46.903856, -98.705817

Stutsman County Courthouse in about 1885, shortly after it was completed. SHSND 1005-0002

The courtroom of the former Stutsman County Courthouse.

Stutsman County Courthouse   145   www.history.nd.gov

Sully's Heart River Corral
STATE HISTORIC SITE

ON JULY 19, 1864, General Alfred Sully led his expedition away from the skeletal outlines of the newly established Fort Rice with a wagon train of immigrants en route to the newly discovered gold fields of Montana (see **Fort Rice**). To continue his pursuit of the Sioux, Sully left the immigrants and a military guard behind at the Heart River. The frightened gold seekers dug rifle pits to protect the wagon train from attack. Remnants of these pits are still visible twenty miles southeast of Richardton, Stark County.

The purpose of the military expedition was to scout the Cannonball River for signs of the Sioux who had escaped from the confrontation at **Whitestone Hill**, but the troops were given the added responsibility of protecting the immigrant train. This angered Sully because the train's slow-moving ox teams impeded the movements of his troops. He also resented the loss of the four hundred soldiers he felt obliged to leave behind for their protection.

Called the "Tom Holmes Expedition" after the man who had organized it, the immigrant train had 123 covered wagons drawn by teams of oxen. The wagons carried between 250 and 500 men, women, and children. A "captain-general" led the train, which was grouped into six divisions, each under its own wagonmaster. A "court" had been elected to deal with any legal matters, and a sheriff, postmaster, and a chaplain served other communal needs.

As the column marched west, rumors of

Indian sightings and impending dangers kept the party watchful. Eventually, the expedition's scouts reported a large encampment of Dakotas at Killdeer Mountain, fifty miles north of the current route.

On the evening of July 24, the expedition reached the Heart River. Sully decided to leave the immigrant train and his own supply train beside the Heart River under the protection of a strong guard. The remainder of the expedition would march quickly to the reported Indian village before the Sioux could escape. Accordingly, July 25 was spent resting men and animals, redistributing supplies, and preparing for the march ahead.

After the departure of the troops on July 26, the people of the wagon train spent five anxious days awaiting the return of Sully's forces. First, they began to fear that a small force of Indians would decoy Sully far away so that the main force could wipe them out and capture the army's supplies. Therefore, the party crossed to the north side of the river and formed the wagons into a corral surrounded by rifle pits and entrenchments. One day the expedition's mules stampeded but were recaptured. On another occasion, nervous guards rousted the men out of their beds at about 11:00 P.M. and called them to the rifle pits where they stood watch for the rest of the night. As a final precaution, the defenders made a "cannon" by hollowing a large log and reinforcing it with iron bands. Several practice shots proved the cannon worked, and all felt a bit safer.

Sully's troops fought the Lakotas, Dakotas, and Yanktonais at Killdeer Mountain and returned to the Heart River encampment on July 31 (see **Killdeer Mountain Battlefield**). Upon their return, the troops spent two days resting while the officers wrote their battle reports and planned the next move. On August 3, Sully's expedition, troops, train and all, again started westward to complete the summer's planned campaign.

Sully's Heart River Corral State Historic Site is small, undeveloped, and lacks a parking lot, directional signs, or any other facilities. It does feature a pristine setting and original rifle pits. A site marker sits in a pasture one-eighth mile east of the road. The rifle pits are to the north and to the east of the marker.

FROM I-94 EXIT #84 AT RICHARDTON, STARK COUNTY

South 12.5 miles on ND-8, east 7.2 miles on 50th St. SW, and north .6 mile on 81st Ave. SW. The site is marked by an aluminum plaque .25 mile east of the road along a farm access road.

GPS 46.696592, -102.154961

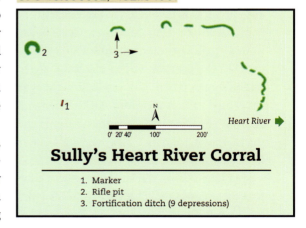

Sully's Heart River Corral

1. Marker
2. Rifle pit
3. Fortification ditch (9 depressions)

Sweden STATE HISTORIC SITE

ESTABLISHED APRIL 28, 1879, the Sweden post office and general store in present-day Walsh County was housed in a log building built by John Magnus Almen, who was the original postmaster. Later that same year, the post office moved to another log building on land owned by William McKenzie, and in January 1880, McKenzie officially replaced Almen as postmaster. The McKenzie enterprise soon expanded to include a livery barn, blacksmith shop, and a new frame house in this growing rural community. In September 1881 the position of postmaster changed hands again when Charles T. Wright was appointed to that position. The Sweden and Grafton post offices were authorized through the efforts of Thomas E. Cooper, who became Grafton's postmaster.

Mail delivery in the late 1800s was a challenging task. Mail was brought to Kelly's Point on the Red River by steamboat from Grand Forks. From there it was carried on horseback by Murdock McKenzie to Grafton and Sweden, a distance of twenty miles. When the Great Northern Railroad extended north from Grafton in 1882, the Sweden post office was discontinued.

All that remains of Sweden is a historical marker erected 450 yards north of its original location, which has been cultivated for many years. The marker can be seen just off North Dakota Highway 9, one and one-fourth miles west of Nash, Walsh County. ◂

FROM NASH, WALSH COUNTY

West 1.5 miles on 73rd St. NE. The site is marked by an aluminum plaque south of the road under two columnar cedar trees.

GPS 48.470289, -97.542737

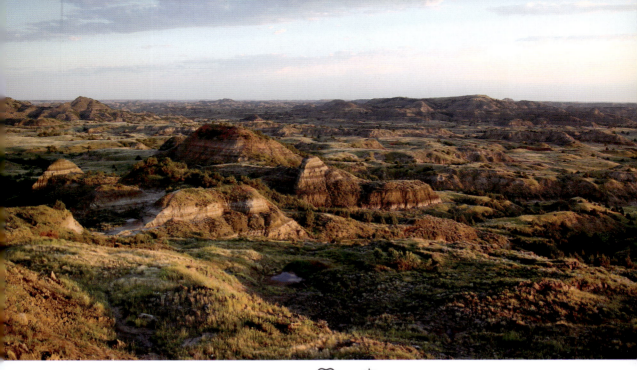

Theodore Roosevelt
NATIONAL PARK

LOCATED IN THE badlands of western North Dakota, Theodore Roosevelt National Park memorializes the twenty-sixth president for his contributions to the conservation of our nation's resources. Roosevelt first came to the badlands in September 1883 to hunt wild game. Before returning to New York two weeks later, he entered into a partnership to raise cattle on the Maltese Cross Ranch. The next year he returned to the badlands and started a second open-range ranch, the Elkhorn. Theodore Roosevelt returned again over the next few years to live the life of a cowboy and explorer, to invigorate his body, and to renew his spirit.

During his time in the badlands, Roosevelt witnessed the virtual disappearance of some big-game species and saw the grasslands almost destroyed by overgrazing. Conservation increasingly became one of Roosevelt's major concerns. During his term as president, Roosevelt founded the US Forest Service and established the first federal game preserve. He created 150 national forests, 51 federal bird reservations, four national game preserves, five national parks, and 24 reclamation projects. His conservation efforts led to the passage of the Antiquities Act, which allows the president to create national monuments. Roosevelt used the act to create eighteen national monuments, preserving and protecting unspoiled places like his beloved badlands as well as other places of significant historical or scientific importance.

The North Dakota badlands provide the scenic backdrop to the park. The various layers of rock that can be seen were deposited between fifty-five and sixty million years ago in what was then a vast lowland swamp east of the young Rocky Mountains. Bentonite, the blue-gray layer of clay, can be traced to ash from ancient volcanoes. Even as these materials were being deposited, streams were cutting through the soft strata. Later, glacial ice sheets blocked the flow of the Little Missouri River and redirected its course near what is now the North Unit of the park. Entrenchment of the river, and a steeper gradient started sculpting the infinite variety of buttes, tablelands, and valleys that made up today's badlands. Fossils of ancient plants and animals are found throughout the park.

The park is home to great variety of living animals and plants. The bison and elk whose disappearance Roosevelt witnessed have been reintroduced and once again roam the park. Herds of feral horses can be seen in the South Unit. Other animals found in the park include mule and white-tailed deer, prairie dogs, and coyotes. Almost 200 species of birds have been observed, including golden and bald eagles. The best viewing hours for wildlife are early morning or late evening. The fifteen inches of precipitation each year support more than 500 different species of plants, including prairie coneflowers, prickly-pear cactus, and trees such as junipers and cottonwoods.

The park is divided into three distinctly different units. The South Unit is located north of Interstate Highway 94 and the town of Medora. Visitor centers at Medora and Painted Canyon offer exhibits, audiovisual programs, book sales, and information. The

Theodore Roosevelt's original Maltese Cross Ranch cabin is now located near the entrance to the south unit. The site of the Elkhorn Ranch, Roosevelt's second ranch in the badlands, is also part of the national park.

A young Theodore Roosevelt poses in buckskins (1884). SHSND 0410-127

A petrified tree in the North Unit of Theodore Roosevelt National Park

Maltese Cross Cabin, Roosevelt's first ranch home, is now located adjacent to the Medora Visitor Center. A scenic loop drive through the park has several turnouts with interpretive signs and overlooks several prairie dog towns. The Ridgeline and Coal Vein nature trails are short, self-guided trails that interpret the geology, ecology, and history of the badlands. Other trails are popular backcountry routes. The 120-mile Maah Daah Hey Trail, open for biking, hiking, and horseback riding, connects the North and South Units of the park and offers breathtaking views. A concessionaire offers trail rides at Peaceful Valley Ranch during the summer. The Medora Visitor Center is open daily year-round, except winter holidays. The Painted Canyon Visitor Center is open daily April through October.

The North Unit has deeper canyons and much more rugged topography. It is located south of Watford City on US Highway 83. The North Unit Visitor Center near the entrance to the park provides exhibits, a store, and information about the park. It is open daily. A fourteen-mile scenic drive through the park has turnouts with interpretive signs and spectacular views overlooking the Little Missouri River. Short, self-guided nature trails interpret the badlands, coulees, and breaks. Other trails lead into the backcountry of the park.

The third section of the park is the Elkhorn Ranch Unit. A one-mile, easy walking trail leads to the site of Roosevelt's "Home Ranch." Although none of the buildings remain, seven exhibits along the path interpret the ranch site through Roosevelt's own words. Considered to be the place many of Roosevelt's conservation ideas were formed, while visiting the site one can still get a sense of the peace and solitude the area provided him. The site is located thirty-five miles north of Medora and is accessible only by gravel and dirt roads.

There are three campgrounds in Theodore National Park. Camping is on a first-come, first-served basis. Use of the North or South Units' group camping sites, or the South Unit's Roundup Horse Camp require advance reservations. Fees are charged for camping in the campgrounds, but free backcountry camping permits are available at the visitor centers. In winter, portions of the park road system in both units may be closed. Information about interpretive programs during the summer can be obtained at the visitor centers.

For further information, write to the Theodore Roosevelt National Park, Box 7, Medora, ND 58654, email thro_interpretation@nps.gov, or call (701) 623-4466 (South Unit) or (701) 842-2333 (North Unit). ◀

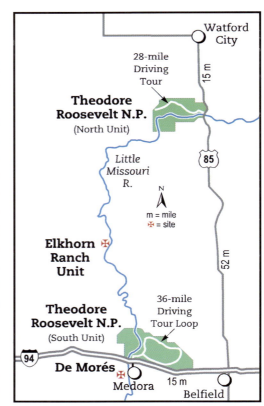

NORTH UNIT: FROM WATFORD CITY, McKENZIE COUNTY
South 15 miles on US-85. The park entrance is north of the highway.
GPS 46.916434, -103.526069

SOUTH UNIT: FROM MEDORA, BILLINGS COUNTY
From the intersection of Pacific Ave. and East River Rd., the park access road is 0.1 mile north on East River Rd.
GPS 47.599537, -103.259597

ELKHORN RANCH UNIT
North 29.5 miles on ND-16, east 12 miles on Blacktail Rd., south 3.25 miles on Belle Lake Rd., and east 2.8 miles on the site access road. The site is unmarked at the end of the road. Ask at the park centers for a map.

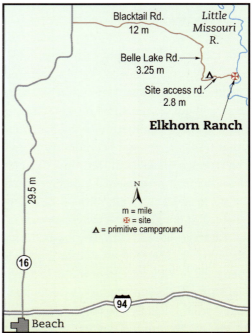

Among the many native species in Theodore Roosevelt National Park is the black-tailed prairie dog.

The site of Theodore Roosevelt's Elkhorn Ranch is show below.

Turtle Effigy STATE HISTORIC SITE

A TURTLE EFFIGY lies on the edge of a high ridge in Mercer County. This effigy is an animal shape formed by arranging stones in a pattern. The turtle feature measures twenty-one feet from head to tail and eleven and one-half feet from side to side. Ninety-five stones are incorporated into the body, which has six appendages: four legs, a head, and a tail. The head is formed from a dense concentration of stones, but the remainder of the body is outlined by a single course of rocks.

Other prehistoric rock figures have been found on the Northern Plains. The outlines include human figures, snakes, geometric patterns, medicine wheels (radiating spokes within a circle), bison, birds, parallel or single boulder lines, connecting lines, triangles, crosses, and oblong or elliptical enclosures. These sites are found in Alberta, Manitoba, Saskatchewan, North Dakota, and South Dakota. Similar turtles in our region have been recorded at Cross Ranch, near Sanger, Oliver County; along the Beulah Trench north of Beulah, Mercer County; northwest of Williston, Williams County; near Ludlow Cave, South Dakota; and on Snake Butte, north of Pierre, South Dakota. Although the actual dates of construction of most of these rock outlines are unknown, the degree of sod cover and the amount of lichen growth on the rocks are clues to their age. The clues suggest that the turtle effigy is at least several hundred years old.

The tribal affiliation of the creators of many of these turtle effigies is unknown. Some tribes, however, such as the Ojibwas, Blackfeet, Dakotas (Sioux), Mandans, and Hidatsas, recognize the importance of the turtle in their religious beliefs and hunting ceremonies. Alfred Bowers, an anthropologist who worked with the Mandans and Hidatsas, attributed many of the turtle effigies to members of these two tribes. He reported that the turtle was used in bison-hunting ceremonies:

> The turtle is also associated with the buffalo on other occasions. Throughout Hidatsa hunting territory are numerous turtle effigies arranged from boulders and situated on high hills with the head pointed toward the river. . . . Nearby are piles of stones on which individual offerings are made to clear the fogs so that the buffalo could be found.[21]

Turtle and other effigies are rare and fragile resources. Vehicle traffic, unauthorized digging, souvenir collection, and cultivation have destroyed many of these sites.

There is not an access road to the Turtle Effigy State Historic Site, which was donated to the state in 1993. For access information, contact the Historic Preservation Division, State Historical Society of North Dakota, 612 East Boulevard Avenue, Bismarck, North Dakota, 58505, or call (701) 328-2666. ◄

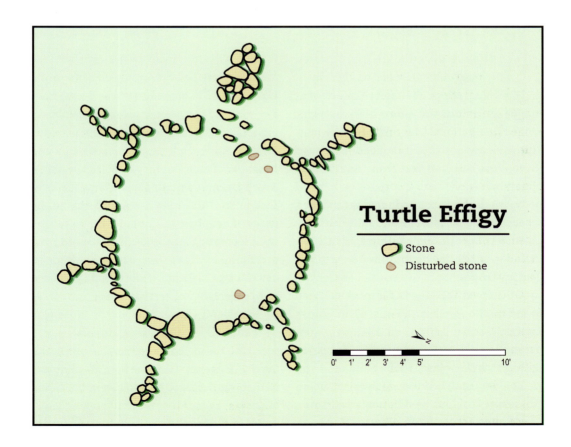

Turtle River STATE PARK

TURTLE RIVER State Park, located twenty miles west of Grand Forks on US Highway 2, is a wonderful example of what can be accomplished when humans work with what is provided by nature—the 784-acre park draws visitors throughout the year to enjoy the seasonal beauty and recreational opportunities.

Turtle River State Park was established through the efforts of former State Historical Society Superintendent Russell Reid. Purchased by the Society in 1933, the property was developed and shaped by the Civilian Conservation Corps (CCC). The CCC was established by Delano Roosevelt's "New Deal" programs which provided relief from unemployment during the Great Depression of the 1930s through work programs for young men and women. The park was originally called Grand Forks State Park, but was later renamed Turtle River State Park.

In 1935 a CCC transient work camp with 185 men was stationed in Larimore to begin work, and later, CCC Companies 764 and 4727 handled most of the labor involved in establishing the park. Construction projects included bridges, roads, parking areas, foot paths and a number of stone and log buildings, many of which are still in use today. Perhaps the most acclaimed CCC project, and still among the park's most popular spots, is the fieldstone dam, swimming area, and bathhouse. The picturesque bath house was converted into the CCC Memorial Picnic Shelter and is a favorite gathering place for large groups.

Woodland Lodge, built in the late 1930s by the CCC, was also a popular park feature used as a dining hall and concessions building. The lodge served as the park's centerpiece until it was damaged by flooding in the spring of 2000. The building was painstakingly dismantled and reconstructed in 2002 on higher ground. The building's old foundation and fieldstone fireplace remain as a reminder of its previous location.

The topography of Turtle River State Park is a departure from what is usually found in the Red River Valley. Ancient glacial Lake Agassiz and its Campbell and McCauleyville beaches are prominent features of the area, while the Turtle River carved out the valley, which is in stark contrast to the soil-rich flatland surrounding the park. Humans were long attracted to the valley, and several archaeological sites are known to be in the park.

The entire park is a nature sanctuary, harboring an abundance of plant and animal life. The river flowing through the park is aptly named for the mud and snapping turtles which inhabit the stream. Wooded areas teaming with squirrels, woodchucks, skunks, weasels, beavers, raccoons, deer, and occa-

Many of the features of Turtle River State Park were constructed by CCC workers under the direction of the State Historical Society in the 1930s. Construction projects included this bridge over the river, Woodland Lodge (above) and the rocked swimming pool (opposite page). Woodland Lodge was reconstructed after the Turtle River flooded in 2000.

sionally a moose can be seen. The wetland, near the park's entrance, is a haven for birds. Diverse vegetation abounds, with much of the area featuring mixed hardwood, timbered hills, and lush river bottoms. Visitors will also find open prairie with wildflowers and native grasses.

Turtle River State Park is open throughout the year, and an entrance fee is charged. A number of rental and picnic facilities, campsites and cabins, hot showers, electrical hookups and a sewage dump station are available from mid-May through September. Activities include hiking, fishing, cross country skiing, downhill sledding, and mountain biking. There are educational offerings each summer weekend at the park's amphitheater. Camping reservations can be made through the North Dakota Parks and Recreation Department website at www.parkrec.nd.gov or by calling (800) 807-4723. More information on the park can also be found on the website or by calling the park directly at (701) 594-4445.

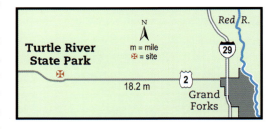

FROM GRAND FORKS, GRAND FORKS COUNTY
West 18.2 miles on US-2. The park entrance is north of the highway.
GPS 47.9387079, -97.4910081

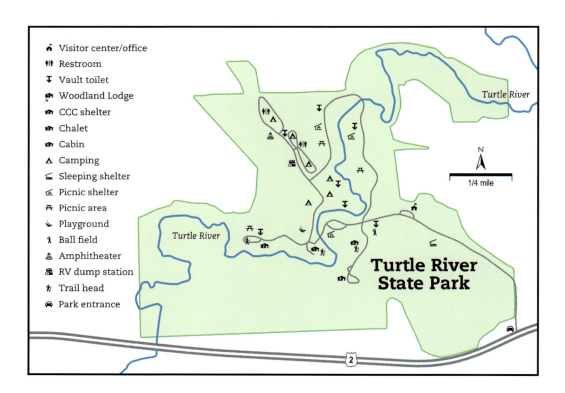

Wadeson Cabin STATE HISTORIC SITE

A HAND-HEWN oak log cabin, with dovetailed corners, stands on its original fieldstone foundation at Wadeson Cabin State Historic Site. It was built in 1876 by Carl Jenson and his nephew Jon Bjerke on the east bank of the Sheyenne River near Kathryn, Barnes County. The cabin has served as a community hall, country store, pioneer home, and, finally, as an icehouse. A marker, beside a small parking area on the north side of the building, presents a short history of the site.

The original cabin contained a single room on the main floor. Later a lean-to was added to the north side, as indicated by a shadow mark (line on the exterior wall) on the gable end. The lean-to is missing. At one time portions of the building were covered with brick-patterned pressed metal, and later the gable ends were protected with tar paper. The only openings in the simple building are a door flanked by a window on the east side, a window on the south side of the main story, and one above in the gable end.

Archaeological excavations uncovered a flagstone threshold in the doorway. Little else was found because of a deep cellar dug when the building was used as an icehouse.

FROM KATHRYN, BARNES COUNTY
From the east end of Main St., southeast and east .8 mile on 51st St. SE. The site is marked by a cabin and an aluminum plaque, on the east side of the Sheyenne River and south of the road.
GPS 46.673352, -97.944859

Walhalla STATE HISTORIC SITE

IN 1842 Henry H. Sibley, American Fur Company trader, sent Norman W. Kittson to Pembina to replace Joseph Rolette Jr. as the head trader in the Red River Valley and International Boundary region. Kittson arrived in 1843 and established three new posts, including one in the vicinity of present-day Walhalla. This post may have been supervised by Antoine B. Gingras (see **Gingras Trading Post**). At about this same time, Rolette helped organize Red River oxcarts into a caravan to haul furs and hides to St. Paul.

The commercial activity generated by the oxcart trade drew many Métis families to the area, and by 1849 there was a resident population of one thousand. In 1852 Kittson moved to the growing community and built a store and warehouse. He was followed by Father George A. Belcourt, who built a chapel dedicated to St. Joseph. The community was subsequently named St. Joseph.

In March 1869 the Hudson's Bay Company surrendered possession of vast acres of land in Manitoba and Saskatchewan to the Dominion of Canada, which effectively eliminated the Métis quest for an independent homeland (the Riel Rebellion). This, along with the opening of a United States land office in December 1870 and the steep decline in the buffalo trade, assured the influx of European immigrants to the St. Joseph area. By 1877 only a handful of Métis lived in St. Joseph and quickly were replaced by Scandinavian immigrants. The town's name was soon changed from St. Joseph to Walhalla at the suggestion of James Wickes Taylor, US Consul and settlement promoter.

In 1899 the Kittson store and warehouse were reportedly serving as stables for the Bellevue Hotel in downtown Walhalla. In hopes of preserving a relic of the fur trade, one of the buildings was dismantled, moved, and rebuilt on its current location at Walhalla State Historic Site in 1904.

Today the log building sits on the edge of the Pembina Escarpment (Hair Hills) overlooking the town of Walhalla. A depression near the southeast edge of the park is reported to be a cellar from one of Alexander Henry's Hair Hills fur trade posts. In 1994 archeological test excavations at the site discovered American Indian pottery dating from 800 to 1700 and Euro-American artifacts dating from the early 1700s to the middle 1800s. A gravel parking lot, restrooms, interpretive sign, and a picnic shelter provide amenities for the visitor. ◄

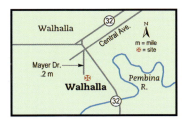

AT WALHALLA, PEMBINA COUNTY

From the intersection of ND-32 and Central Ave., south .2 mile on Martyr Drive. The site is marked by an aluminum plaque and a cabin at the end of the road.

GPS 48.917684, -97.922360

Norman Kittson founded the American Fur Company post at Pembina in 1843. Minnesota Historical Society image

Welk Homestead

THE WELK HOMESTEAD, located northwest of Strasburg, interprets agriculture in the early 19th century, German-Russian culture and architecture, and the career of bandleader Lawrence Welk, who grew up on the farm.

The 6.11 acre site is the homestead of Ludwig and Christina Welk, who immigrated from near Odessa, Russia, in 1893. Nearly 120,000 people of German heritage left Russia for the US between 1870 and 1920, mainly due to political pressures. Free or cheap land drew many to North Dakota, where they settled mainly in the south central counties of Emmons, Logan, and McIntosh. See map of German settlement in North Dakota on page 186.

The house was built in 1899 of dried mud brick known as *batsa*, a common construction method of the Germans from Russia both on the Russian steppe and the North American prairie. Other architectural features also point to the family's German-Russian heritage. A summer kitchen, outhouse, blacksmith shop, and granary, as well as a barn, which was moved onto the site about 1949, are also open seasonally.

The Welk family grew wheat and other crops, raised chickens to sell eggs, and kept cows to sell cream. Their sixth child, Lawrence Welk, was born March 11, 1903. He learned to play the accordion from his father and attended the local Catholic school, where classes were conducted in German. Lawrence left the farm in 1924 to pursue a career in music. In 1955 he made his debut on national television. The Lawrence Welk Show was produced for twenty-six years, and reruns can still be seen throughout the country as well as internationally.

Ludwig and Christina Welk retired to Strasburg in 1928, and their youngest son Michael and his family operated the farm until 1965. The Welk homestead is located just off Highway 83 at 845 88th Street Southeast, Strasburg, North Dakota, 58573.

FROM STRASBURG, EMMONS COUNTY
North .8 mile on US-83, west 2 miles on 88th St. SE, north .3 mile and east .2 mile to the site. The homestead is at the end of the road.
GPS 46.150277, -100.207881

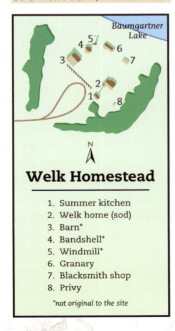

Lawrence Welk, with his famous accordion, early 1920s. SHSND C3600

Whitestone Hill
STATE HISTORIC SITE

LOCATED JUST WEST of the James River Valley, Whitestone Hill State Historic Site is listed in the National Register of Historic Places. The area around Whitestone Hill has been sacred to Native Americans for hundreds of years. Tribes met here in large groups to visit, trade, arrange marriages, conduct ceremonies, organize fall bison hunts, and prepare for the winter. Fresh water, berries, prairie turnips, chokecherries, and other resources were nearby. Whitestone Hill also marks the scene in September 1863 of the fiercest attack by US soldiers on Sioux people in North Dakota, part of the military excursions following the US-Dakota War of 1862 in Minnesota (See **Sibley's and Sully's Northwest Indian Campaigns**).

The James River Valley had been home to the Yanktonai and Cuthead people since they broke off from their parent nation, the Dakotas, in Minnesota sometime before the year 1600. The valley had become the major trade center of the bands. In the summer of 1863 the Yanktonais, Isantis, Blackfeet, and Hunkpapas came together for an intertribal buffalo hunt. A number of prominent Yanktonai leaders had brought bands to the gathering, including Nasúna Thaŋká (Big Head) and Mahtó Nuŋpa (Two Bears). The Hunkpapa chief Wí Sápa (Black Moon) was also present. Some Dakota refugees from Minnesota were also there as part of the camp of about 3,000 people. Whether any of these Dakota people had participated in the Minnesota conflict is still disputed.

Major Albert E. House of the 6th Iowa Cavalry, leading a scouting party in advance of General Sully's forces, discovered the encampment by a lake near Whitestone Hill on the morning of September 23. He immediately sent soldiers to notify General Sully and request reinforcements. While they were gone, the Indians detected the presence of the troops. Some of the villagers prepared to flee, and others prepared to fight. For nearly three hours, an uneasy standoff continued, during which a delegation of Sioux elders approached the soldiers. Some of the elders offered to surrender themselves to protect their people. House, however, insisted on total surrender, and negotiations broke down.

Sully's command was less than a mile away when the villagers saw them coming, and departure preparations became frantic. Tipis were stripped, travois were hastily attached to ponies and dogs, and possessions and small children were strapped to the travois. Masses of Indians began streaming east, down a ravine that opened into a shallow mouth at the rear of the village. Some young children were strapped by their parents to the backs of horses or the large village dogs and chased away, in the hope that they would escape.

It was nearly sunset when Sully's troops reached the scouting party, and as the main column advanced toward the village, it became apparent that people were escaping. Sully ordered Colonel Robert W. Furnas, commanding the 2nd Nebraska Cavalry, forward at full speed to cut off the Indians' retreat. Stopping briefly to instruct Major House to circle around to the left (north and east), Furnas directed his men around to the right (south), hoping to encircle the village. Seeing that Whitestone Hill blocked escape to the south, Sully sent Colonel Wilson with troops to the north side of the village.

General Sully, with one company of the 7th Iowa Cavalry, two companies of the Sixth Iowa Cavalry, and the artillery battery, charged toward the center of the village. As they passed through the village, they captured a number of prisoners, who were left behind under guard. Sully and his troops climbed to the top of Whitestone Hill to direct the rest of the battle and to offer artillery support, if needed by the soldiers on the flats below.

Most of the villagers tried to escape down the ravine. They began to gather in a large throng at a broadening of the ravine about one-half mile from the village, where they were surrounded by soldiers.. Fearing that the Indians might escape in the impending darkness, Furnas ordered his men to dismount and advance toward the ravine on foot. When his men were within a few hundred yards, he ordered them to begin firing, and other troops followed his lead. Soldiers were firing down upon the mass of men, women, and children from both banks of the ravine, wounding and killing many. Wilson's troops remained mounted, and as the attack continued, their horses became unmanageable, allowing the warriors to break through the line and create a space for their families to escape.

As darkness deepened, Colonel Furnas saw that bullets from the other units were hitting his lines. He withdrew his troops to higher ground surrounding the ravine. Other units also stopped firing and spent the night on the hilltops overlooking the destroyed village.

The light of day revealed a field of carnage. Dead and wounded men, women, and children, lay in the campsite and in the ravine. Tipis stood vacant, or drooped in vari-

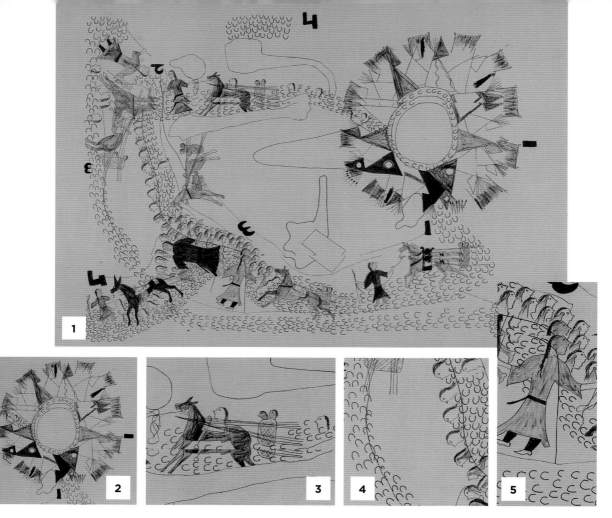

Around 1914 or 1915, Waháčhaŋka Ikíkču (Takes His Shield), a Yanktonai survivor of Whitestone Hill, explained his view of the events. Richard Cottonwood created a map or picture of events as retold by Takes His Shield. In 1932, Aaron McGaffey Beede, an attorney and former missionary to Standing Rock who had talked to Takes His Shield about the pictograph, wrote an interpretation and created a blueprint copy, which was sent to the State Historical Society. Takes His Shield's pictograph is one of the few known primary source documents available that tell the Sioux experience at Whitestone. A small version of the pictograph, and a very brief summary of the description, is presented here. The full image and the complete description is available at http://ndstudiestest.nd.gov/content/whitestone-hill-pictograph-0. Interested readers are encouraged to study the entire document.

(1) Many people were gathered at the camp on the autumn bison hunt and were drying meat for the winter, shown by the tipis and the meat drying racks. The horse tracks of white solders are shown swooping upon the camp. (2) The Sioux flee from the soldiers, and a fleeing woman has attached a travois carrying two children to a horse. (3) A little later the horseshoes of the soldiers show that they have the Indians between them and are shooting them, and many were killed. (4) Some of the people escape alive. (5) XXX

ous stages of destruction. Camp equipment and personal items, tools, utensils, weapons, toys, and injured or dying horses and dogs littered the ground. Injured women protected babies and little children. While some squads of soldiers patrolled the region searching for escapees, other men were put to work digging graves and destroying the village and Indian possessions. J. J. Worley of the 2nd Nebraska Regiment described the events of September 4 in a letter: "In the morning the sight was hard to behold. Both Indians (men, women and children), and soldiers and their horses, lay strewn over the field, and piled up on each other. The Indians' property lay strewn over six or seven miles. . . . That day was spent in burying our dead and shooting their dogs and wounded Indians, and capturing ponies and plunder."[22]

Sully reported that twenty soldiers were killed (including two killed several days later) and thirty-eight soldiers were wounded, some from "friendly fire." Although there was no accurate count of the Indian casualties, estimates ranged from 100 to 300 dead. In addition, thirty-two men and 124 women and children were captured. For two days, military patrols guarded against reprisal raids while troops destroyed Indian property. Tipis, buffalo hides, wagons, travois, blankets, and perhaps as much as a half million pounds of buffalo meat prepared for winter were burned. Troops threw pots, kettles, weapons, and other things that would sink into the lake.

On September 5, one of the scouting details ran into a party of Indians. In the ensuing skirmish, two more white soldiers were killed. The following day, Sully and his army marched south toward their transport on the Missouri River. The Indians who had escaped the soldiers scattered over the plains looking for friends and families who could share necessities during the winter months.

The Yanktonai people prior to Whitestone had been a strong tribe with a vigorous trade network and had not clashed with US Army troops. After the battle, they were prisoners or refugees fleeing to relatives in Canada, Montana, and elsewhere. They never returned to their homeland, but the events that caused their scattering remained vivid in their memories. Napé Ȟóta Wiŋ (Mary Big Moccasin) was nine years old when she was shot by soldiers at Whitestone. Her descendents say that many years later, as an old woman, she still had

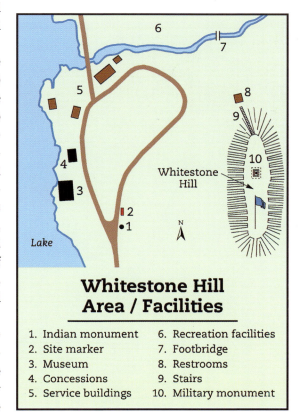

Whitestone Hill Area / Facilities

1. Indian monument
2. Site marker
3. Museum
4. Concessions
5. Service buildings
6. Recreation facilities
7. Footbridge
8. Restrooms
9. Stairs
10. Military monument

nightmares about Whitestone, crying "Run, Run," because the soldiers were coming.[23]

Today, Whitestone Hill State Historic Site includes a portion of the 1863 village site and area of the attack. There are two monuments, one honoring the Sioux and a second commemorating the soldiers. A fieldstone shelter beside the trail provides a resting point overlooking a freshwater lake. Nearby is a picnic area with a shelter, table, pit toilets, and a parking lot. Admission is free, and donations are accepted. ◂

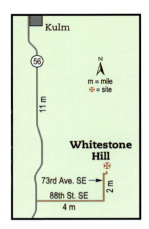

FROM KULM, LAMOURE COUNTY
South 11 miles on ND-56, east 4 miles on 88th St. SE, and north 2 miles on 73rd Ave. SE to the site gate. The site is located to the east of the lake.
GPS 46.168909, -98.856820

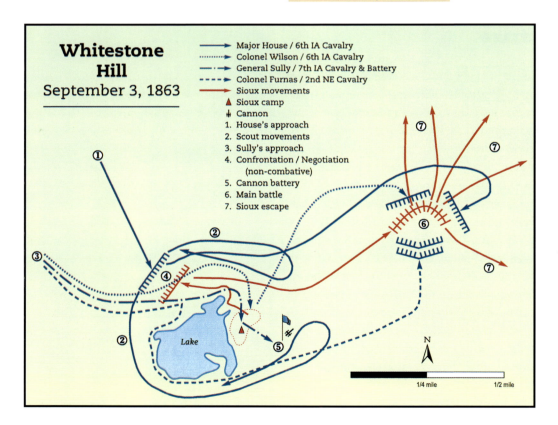

Writing Rock STATE HISTORIC SITE

TWO GRANITE BOULDERS inscribed with thunderbird figures are exhibited at Writing Rock State Historic Site in Divide County, which is north of Grenora (Williams County). The designs on the rocks are clearly American Indian, despite unfounded speculation attributing the origins of the "mysterious carvings" to Vikings, Chinese, or others. Similar rock art sites are found in Roch Percée and Kamsack, Saskatchewan; Long-view and Writing-on-Stone Provincial Park, Alberta; Pictograph Cave near Billings, Montana; Dinwoody, Wyoming; Ludlow Cave, South Dakota; and at numerous archaeological sites in the upper Midwestern United States.

Thunderbirds, mythological creatures responsible for lightning and thunder, are central to stories told by Algonquian and Siouan-speaking tribes. Many Plains Indians such as the Plains Cree, Plains Ojibwa, Gros Ventre, Crows, Dakotas, Mandans, and Hidatsas used thunderbirds in their art. The design appears on prehistoric artifacts such as shell and bone pendants and pottery, as well as on rock art. Most of these artifacts on the Northern Plains date from A.D. 1000 to A.D. 1700.

The larger of the two granite boulders measures four and one-half feet high and four feet wide. A massive, flying bird surrounded by interconnected lines and circles covers the flattest side of the boulder. The second, smaller rock is three and one-half feet long, two feet wide, and one and one-half feet high. It displays a smaller, flying bird connected to circles and abstract lines. A second bird, which is missing its head, flies above the other designs. All of the motifs were pecked by pounding a hard rock against the boulders or were ground into the surfaces.

The smaller rock was originally located some distance from the larger one and was once removed from the site but later returned. Today, the two boulders are enclosed in a shelter and protected by iron bars at the historic site. Recreational facilities at the historic site include picnic tables in a grove of trees, picnic shelters, a building with a kitchen, fireplace, playground equipment, restrooms, and a parking lot. ◄

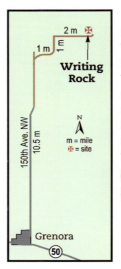

FROM GRENORA, WILLIAMS COUNTY
North 10.5 miles on 150th Ave. NW to a right fork, east 1 mile, north 1 mile, and east 2 miles. The site is marked by a shelter at the end of the road.

GPS 48.780797, -103.858652

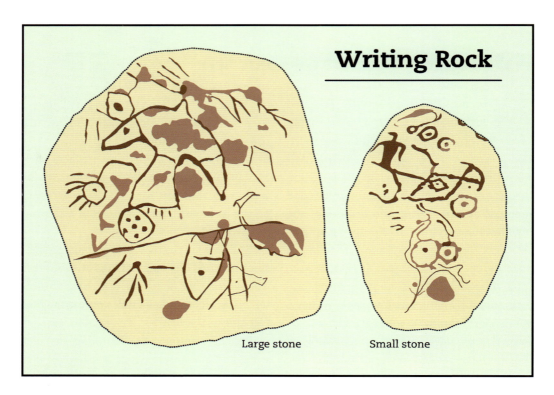

Writing Rock

Large stone

Small stone

Sibley's and Sully's Northwest Indian Campaigns

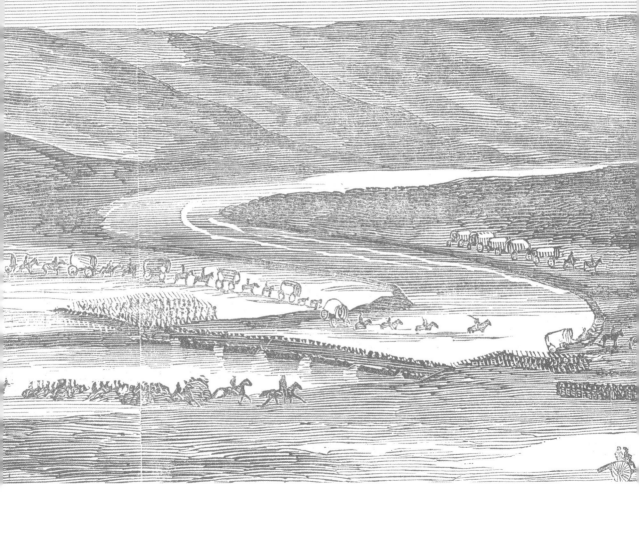

THE NORTHWEST INDIAN CAMPAIGNS grew out of the US-Dakota War of 1862, an event sometimes classified as part of the US Civil War and sometimes as the beginning of the Indian Wars. The conflict began on August 18, 1862, when small groups of Dakota warriors raided white settlers living in southern Minnesota.

The Dakotas of southern Minnesota were frustrated by years of accumulated grievances against white settlers and government officials over issues relating to reservation lands and controversial administrative practices. In the preceding decade the Dakotas, who had once controlled much of what was now the state of Minnesota, had been forced to cede almost all their land in the state, retaining only a small strip south of the Minnesota River. The Dakotas were further provoked when annuity goods and cash from the US government, promised in exchange for the land cessions, were delayed. Fearing starvation after a poor harvest, and knowing government warehouses were full of food, some frustrated and angry Mdewakanton and Wahpekute Dakotas attacked farms, several settlements, Fort Ridgely along the Minnesota River in southwestern Minnesota, and Fort Abercrombie on the Red River of the North (see **Fort Abercrombie State Historic Site**). Most Dakotas did not join in, some choosing to aid and protect settlers, while others attempted to stay out of the conflict. Some were not even present, but were hunting in the lands west of the Red River. An estimated 450 to 800 settlers and soldiers were killed in these attacks; Dakota losses were estimated at about twenty-one.

Although approximately 40,000 white settlers fled during the initial stages of the con-flict, within a few days, locally raised militia began fighting back. Due to the demands of the raging Civil War, few "regular" US troops were available for frontier service. The available state militia troops were mostly young, poorly trained, and poorly armed. However, at Wood Lake, these soldiers under the command of Colonel Henry Hastings Sibley won a significant victory, ending the fighting and raiding in Minnesota.

As the military arrested suspected perpetrators, many Dakotas, participants and non-participants alike, feared retaliation and fled to other areas. It was reported that Thaóyate Dúta (Little Crow), a principal Mdewakanton leader of the conflict, and Inkpáduta (Scarlet Point), a hostile Wahpekute leader, had retreated to the vicinity of Devils Lake in Dakota Territory. Others fled to other parts of Dakota Territory or to Canada. Eventually, nearly four hundred Dakotas were tried by a military tribunal for their alleged participation in the conflict; of these, 308 were sentenced to hang. President Abraham Lincoln commuted many of the death sentences, but thirty-eight of those convicted were hanged at Mankato, Minnesota, on December 26, 1862.

Still, many Minnesotans wanted further retribution, including removal of all the Dakotas from Minnesota and continued arrests of escaped perpetrators. The distinction between Dakotas who had participated in the fighting and those who had not began to blur. Some believed that future hostilities could be prevented only if severe punishment continued, and that the prospect of a new outbreak was likely. Approximately eight hundred Dakotas had fled the Lower Sioux reservation, and there were another 4,000 Dakotas at the

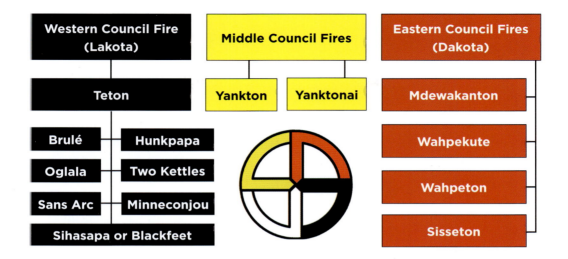

OČHÉTI ŠAKÓWIŊ ▶ SEVEN COUNCIL FIRES OF THE DAKOTA

The word Dakȟóta means "friend" or "relative" and is the name the Dakota people call themselves. They are also often called the Sioux, a name given to them by other tribes. It is sometimes interpreted as meaning "snake" or may come from a phrase that means "those who speak another language."

Historically there were seven major groups of the Dakota Nation, known as the Seven Council Fires. Each group lived in a particular area, but often met with others to hunt or for celebrations.

The four eastern council fires are the Bdewákhathuŋwaŋ (Mdewakanton), Waȟpékhute (Wahpekute), Sisíthuŋwaŋ (Sisseton), and Waȟpéthuŋwaŋ (Wahpeton). They lived in what is now southern Minnesota and northern Iowa and practiced agriculture. These four are also called the Dakotas.*

The two council fires of the Iȟáŋkthuŋwaŋ (Yanktons) and Iȟáŋkthuŋwaŋna (Yanktonais) lived to the west of the Dakotas. They practiced agriculture as well as hunting.

To the west of the Missouri River was the council fire of the Lakȟóta.** The seven bands that comprise the Lakotas are the Sičháŋǧu (Brulé), Oglála (Oglala), Itázipčho (Sans Arc), Húŋkpapȟa (Hunkpapa), Mnikȟówožu (Minneconjou), Sihásapa (Sihasapa or Black Feet), and the Oóhenuŋpa (Two Kettles).

In this book we will be as specific in describing a group as possible. However, we will use the term Dakota if describing a mixed group of Mdewakanton, Wahpekute, Sisseton, or Wahpeton people. We will use the term Lakota when we cannot specifically identify people as Hunkpapa, Sans Arc, or one of the other Lakota bands or when a number of bands are gathered together. When the records are unclear or refer to a mixed group of Dakotas, Yantonais, and Lakotas we will use the term Sioux.

---

*They are also known as the **Isáŋyathi** (Santee).
They are also known as the **Thítȟuŋwaŋ (Teton).

General Alfred Sully. SHSND C0251-0001

scientists, and soldiers had been expounding the many values and assets of the upper Missouri region. Enough information had been gathered to suggest that fortunes could be made. By 1861 land companies were already offering potential town sites and farms for sale in parts of the region. Steamboats and wagon trains, filled with miners, merchants, and families headed toward the gold fields of Montana and Idaho, and it was known that a transcontinental railroad would be crossing these plains once the Civil War ended. Military control of the territory would aid all these possibilities.

General Pope's plan called for one army to march from Minnesota to the Devils Lake area, engaging the Sioux along the way, or pushing them westward towards the Missouri River. Meanwhile, a second army would advance northward along the Missouri, preventing escape across the river. Those caught between

more northern reservation, many of whom had vacated their villages and moved further into eastern Dakota Territory. Also, it was feared that thousands of Yanktons and Yanktonai from the eastern plains of Dakota Territory might rise up in support of their Minnesota relatives. Therefore, General John Pope, recently appointed commander of the new Military Department of the Northwest, devised a plan to trap the enemy Sioux in Dakota Territory.

The stated reason for Pope's decision to mount a major military campaign into Dakota Territory was his perception of a real danger of further Indian attacks on the still-nervous frontier. There also may have been other military, economic, and political considerations. The fur trade had reached the Missouri River by 1792, and a succession of traders, explorers,

General Henry Hastings Sibley. SHSND A3200

the two armies would either be captured or killed. The two armies were scheduled to rendezvous on July 25, 1863, at the Missouri River, where the field commanders could determine further action.

Sibley, who had displayed outstanding leadership as a colonel of volunteers during the conflict, was appointed to lead the Minnesota arm of the joint campaign. He was a veteran fur trader and knew the Dakota people well. As a former governor of Minnesota, General Sibley was well known and respected. General Alfred Sully, a West Point graduate experienced in Indian campaigns, was eventually chosen to command the second army

The country through which Sibley and Sully marched was occupied; Native Americans had lived in and made use of this land for thousands of years. The region was divided into fluid territories in which particular groups could claim dominance for extended periods of time. The Native American groups and their approximate territories as they existed in the late 1850s and early 1860s are identified in the map on pages 182–183. In general much of the eastern portion of what would be North Dakota was claimed by the Dakotas. The Yanktonais claimed much of the land between the James and Missouri Rivers. Lakotas ranged across the lands west of the Missouri. None of these areas were occupied by one group exclusively. Many Dakotas and Lakotas had joined their Yanktonai relatives hunting for buffalo. Sibley and Sully would encounter members of all these groups as they marched across the territory.

Sibley's forces reached Dakota Territory near Big Stone Lake on June 24, 1863. They entered present-day North Dakota on July 2 southeast of Lake Tewaukon and headed

Tȟatȟáŋka Nážin (Standing Buffalo), a Sisseton chief, had tried to keep his people out of the US-Dakota War of 1862. At the time the conflict started he and many of his followers were hunting buffalo in Dakota. Standing Buffalo was one of the leaders present at Big Mound. SHSND A0138-0002

northwest towards Devils Lake (see **Camp Buell, Camp Weiser, Camp Sheardown,** and **Camp Corning**). By July 17 Sibley had learned that the fugitive Sioux had left the Devils Lake area and were moving toward the Missouri River. In order to increase his army's mobility, Sibley deposited unneeded baggage, surplus supplies, and disabled men and animals at Camp Atchison and continued the pursuit at a faster pace (see **Camp Atchison, Camp Kimball,** and **Camp Grant,** and **Lake Johnson**).

Sibley's and Sully's Northwest Indian Campaign

Phizí (Gall), a Hunkpapa leader, was a close associate of Sitting Bull. He fought at both Big Mound and Killdeer. He was photographed with his young nephew by D. F. Barry, circa 1885. SHSND A1624

After battles on July 24 at Big Mound (see **Big Mound Battlefield** and **McPhail's Butte Overlook** and **Camp Whitney**), July 26 at Dead Buffalo Lake, and July 28 at Stony Lake, Sibley pursued the Sioux to the Missouri. Native warriors engaged Sibley's troops as their families successfully escaped across the river on July 30. After waiting two more days in hopes of a rendezvous with General Sully's troops, Sibley, his command short of food and his men exhausted, returned to Camp Atchison. On August 12, 1863, they headed home to Minnesota (see **Camp Arnold**, **Buffalo Creek**, and **Maple Creek Crossing**).

While Sibley waited for Sully at the Missouri River, Sully waited for his steamboats at Fort Pierre (at present-day Pierre, South Dakota). Sully's arm of the campaign was plagued by a succession of delays. The biggest factor in the command's late departure was a prolonged drought that prevented the expedition's steamboats from moving on the uncommonly low water levels of the Missouri River. On the July 25 rendezvous date, Sully's troops had just arrived at Fort Pierre and were still three weeks ahead of the steamboats. In mid-August, Sully, desperate to advance, loaded the available supplies onto borrowed wagons and marched overland toward Devils Lake with rations adequate for a mere twenty-three days.

In late August, long after Sibley had departed for Minnesota, Sully's command reached Long Lake, southeast of present-day Bismarck. Realizing that he had missed Sibley, Sully still hoped to catch up with the Sioux. Captured informants reported that the Sioux had escaped Sibley's army by crossing the Missouri, but had returned after Sibley departed and had moved eastward to hunt buffalo for winter provisions. Sully turned his army eastward toward the James River.

On September 3, 1863, a scouting party discovered an Indian village near Whitestone Hill. The soldiers stalled the Indians' escape long enough for Sully to bring his main force into battle position. The confrontation at Whitestone Hill is considered to be the bloodiest attack by whites on native Americans in eastern North Dakota. Twenty-three soldiers and an estimated one hundred to three hundred Indians were killed, including many women and children. Another 158 people were captured, and most of the their food, shelter, tools, weapons, and transportation were destroyed, leaving the survivors destitute in the face of the coming winter (see **Whitestone Hill**). With his mission essentially accomplished and supplies dangerously low, Sully and his men returned to winter quarters, thus ending the 1863 field campaign.

In 1864 General Sully returned to the Upper Missouri, establishing **Fort Rice** on July 7, 1864. Almost two weeks later he led his

Mahtó Nuŋpa (Two Bear) was photographed with other Yanktonai chiefs by Stanley Morrow in about 1870. He is standing in the far left, back row. Two Bear was one of the Yanktonai leaders at Whitestone Hill. SHSND 0670-011

Maȟpíya Bogawiŋ (Gathering of Clouds Woman), also known as Nellie Gates, was the daughter of the Yanktonai Chief Mahtó Nuŋpa (Two Bear). She was born in 1854 and witnessed the attack at Whitestone Hill. A highly skilled beadwork artist, she later recorded her memories of Whitestone Hill on a beadwork satchel like the one in this photograph. SHSND 1952-3240-2

expedition away from the new fort, escorting a wagon train of gold seekers en route to Montana. Learning of the presence of a large group of Sioux, Sully left the immigrants behind at **Sully's Heart River Corral** and proceeded to **Killdeer Mountain**, where a large village of mostly Lakota and Yanktonai people were attacked, many killed, and winter supplies destroyed. Returning to the Heart River encampment, Sully led his troops and the wagon train west to the Yellowstone River, crossing the Badlands. Warriors from Killdeer attacked and harassed the column in retaliation, taking advantage of the Badlands landscape. As Sully and his men struggled west to the Missouri River, where they expected to find steamboats with supplies, the Sioux engaged them in a running skirmish known as the Battle of the Badlands. Low on food and water for animals

Colonel Robert Furnas of the 2nd Nebraska Cavalry and his staff officers (front), Furnas, Lt. Col. W. F. Sapp, Dr. A. Bowen and Major George Armstrong; (rear) Major John Taffe, Major John Pearman, and Adj. Henry Atkinson. The 2nd Nebraska Cavalry fought at Whitestone Hill. SHSND SA 10548-V1-p34

force of cavalry journeyed again through much of the region they had crossed the year before. This time Sully encountered few Indians and fought no battles, The Dakota military campaigns of the 1860s had ended.

The results of these campaigns were far-reaching. From the perspective of the Euro-American participants, confidence in the security of southern Minnesota and eastern Dakota Territory was restored. Thousands of young men became aware of the fertile lands that could be claimed by a new crop of potential settlers. Growing commercial, agricultural, and transportation endeavors east of the Missouri River were enhanced by the newfound security.

For the Sioux, the events of 1863–65 permanently changed their way of life. Men, women, and children were killed, and the supplies needed to sruvive the winter were de-

and men, the soldiers reached the steamboats on August 12 and headed downstream to Fort Union, near the junction of the Yellowstone and Missouri Rivers. Lacking sufficient horses or supplies, and with his soldiers exhausted, Sully ended the campaign and returned down river. The final conflict ignited by the 1864 Sully campaign occurred in September, when Lakota warriors encountered another wagon train crossing their territory, resulting in the siege of **Fort Dilts**. In 1865 Sully and a small

Tȟatȟáŋka Ská (White Bull), a Hunkpapa chief and nephew of Sitting Bull, defended the village at Killdeer when it was attacked by Sully. This photograph was taken many years later by Frank Fiske at Fort Yates, North Dakota. SHSND 1952-6176

stroyed. Bands and family groups of Dakotas and Yanktonais, many of whom had not been involved in the original Minnesota warfare, were scattered and forced to leave ancestral homes and traditional hunting grounds. Tribal politics and leadership as well as family relationships were disrupted.

Many Indians located west of the river had also been drawn into the military campaigns. They did not suffer the level of destruction faced by the eastern Sioux but were angered by the military intrusions. These more westerly tribes were facing their own issues, as gold seekers and others crossed their lands. The events of the Sibley and Sully campaigns escalated these intrusions and foreshadowed future conflict. The Indian-white warfare initiated in Minnesota in 1862 continued sporadically on the Northern Plains for another twenty-seven years. ◄

In July 1864 Joseph and Fanny Kelly were traveling by wagon train through what is now Wyoming when their party was attacked by Oglala warriors and Fanny Kelly was captured. Kelly was present in the village at Killdeer when it was attacked by Sully's men. She was eventually freed in December and later wrote a book about her experiences, Narrative of My Captivity Among the Sioux Indians. *SHSND 0200-6x8-0308*

Maȟtó Watȟápa, or John Grass, was a leader of the Sihasapa warriors who besieged the Fort Dilts wagon train. This photograph was taken about 1890 by D. F. Barry. SHSND C0222

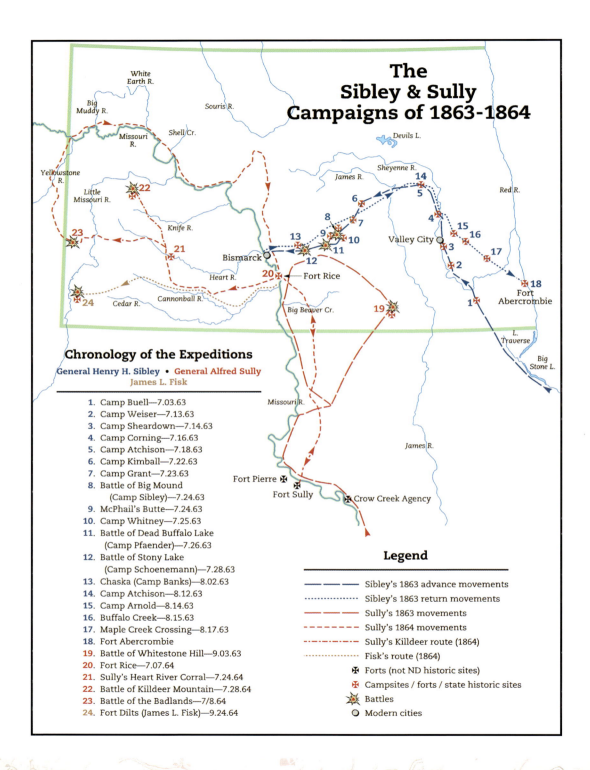

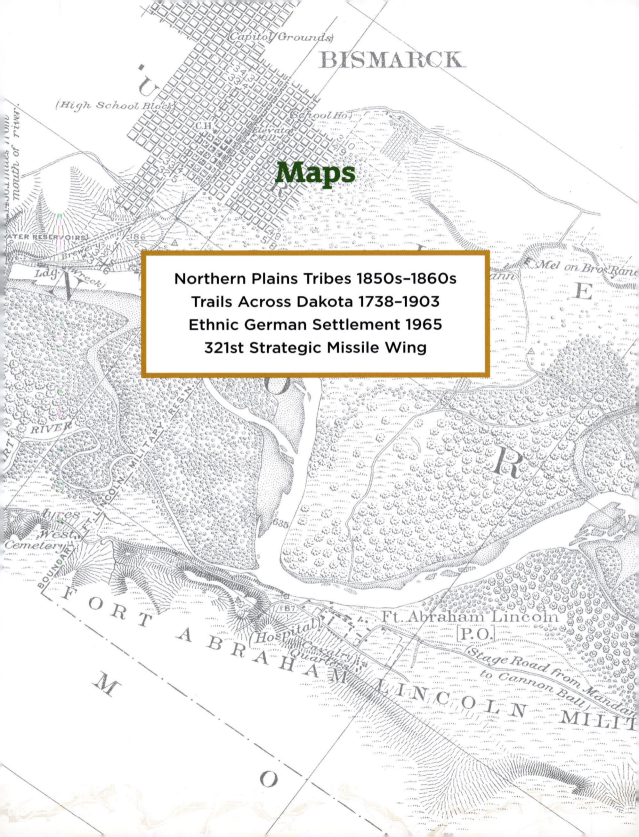

Maps

Northern Plains Tribes 1850s–1860s
Trails Across Dakota 1738–1903
Ethnic German Settlement 1965
321st Strategic Missile Wing

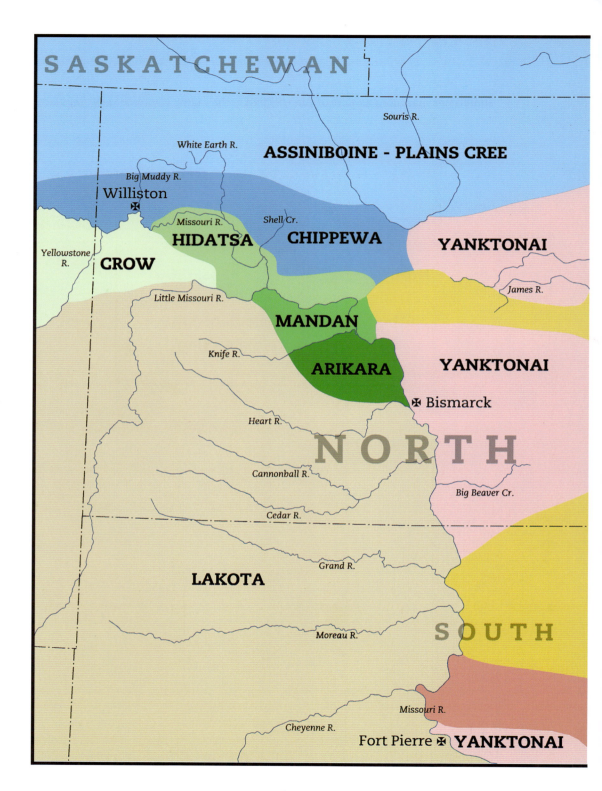

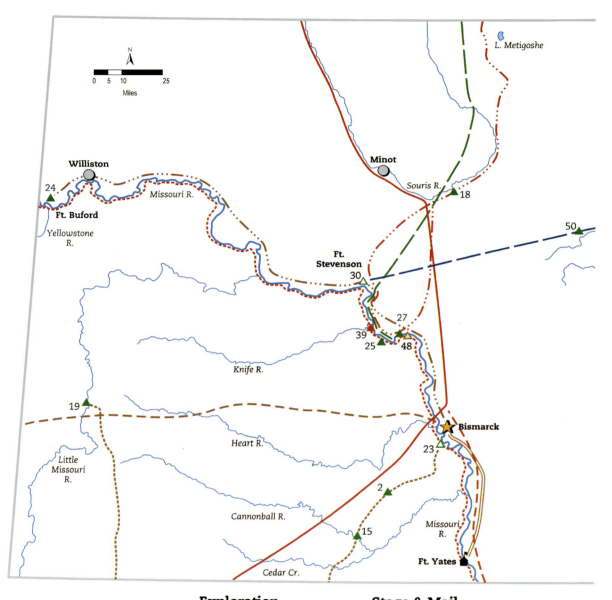

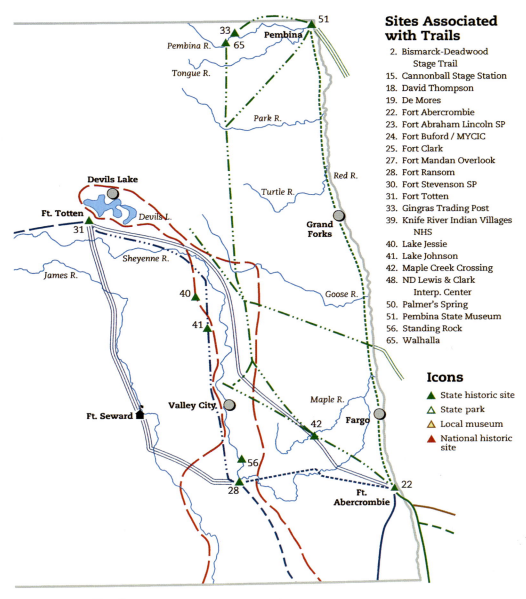

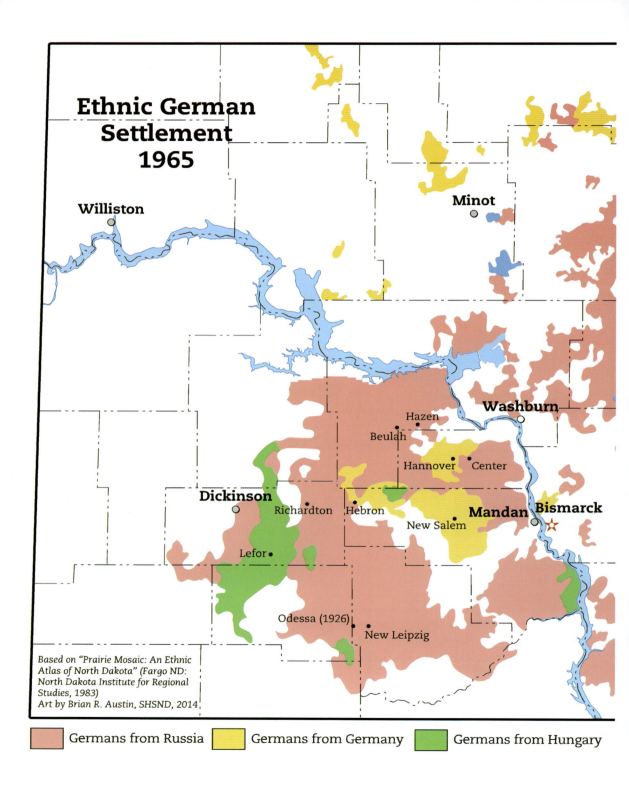

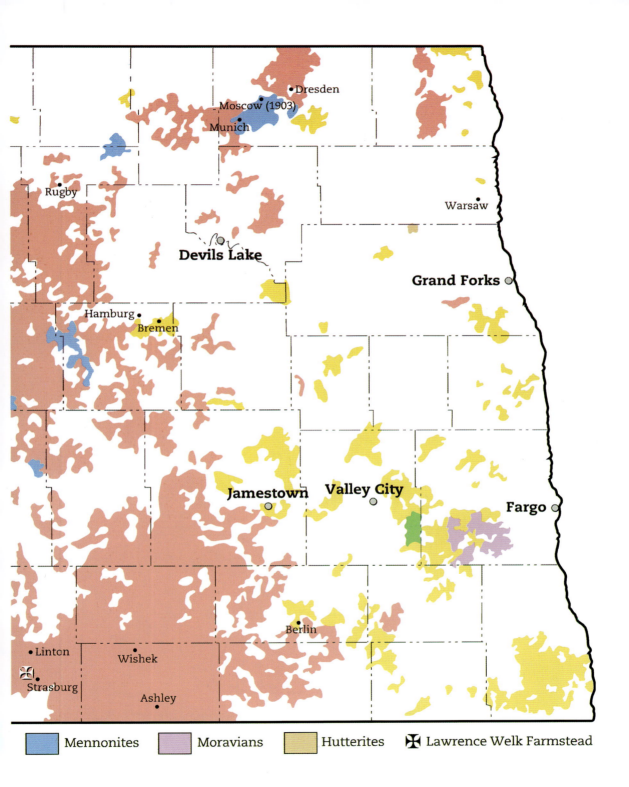

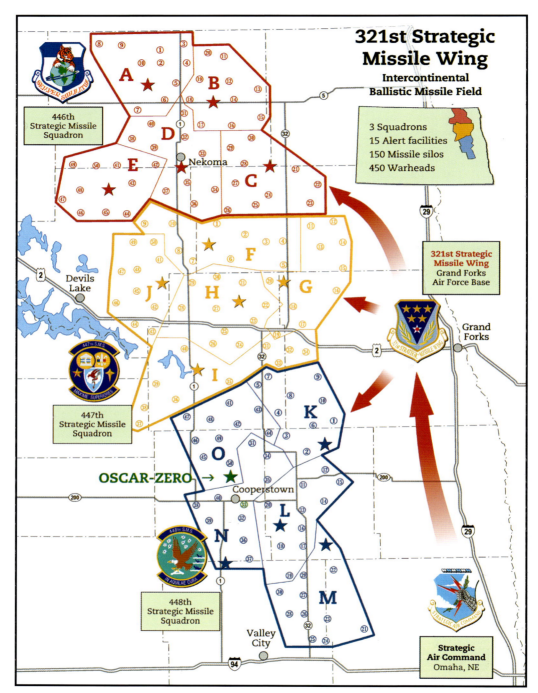

Refer to the Ronald Reagan Minuteman Missile State Historic Site on page 132.

Endnotes

1. Gary Anderson and Alan Woolworth, eds., *Through Dakota Eyes* (St. Paul: Minnesota Historical Society Press, 1988), 283.

2. Charles Alexander Eastman, *Indian Boyhood* (Boston: Little, Brown, 1929; reprint, Glorieta, NM: Rio Grande Press, Inc., 1976), 14.

3. Enoch M. Eastman diary, July 3, 1863, Camp Buel [sic]. Enoch M. Eastman Papers. MSS 20010, State Historical Society of North Dakota (SHSND). Eastman was a teamster and a member of Company E, Hatch's Battalion, Minnesota, Volunteer Cavalry, 1865.

4. "Diary of Unknown Soldier, June 16-August 27, 1863," July 3, 1863. Sibley Expedition Collection. MSS 10386, SHSND.

5. O[scar] G[arrett] Wall diary, July 23, 1863. MSS 20181. SHSND. Wall was a civilian on the Sibley Expedition with the 5th Regiment, Minnesota Volunteer Infantry.

6. L. B. Smith diary, July 23, 1863. MSS 20839. SHSND. Smith was a surgeon with the 7th Regiment, Minnesota Volunteers.

7. George C. Pettie diary, July 23, 1863. MSS 20559. SHSND. Pettie belonged to Company A, 10th Regiment, Minnesota volunteer Infantry, Steele County, Minnesota.

8. John Danielson, "The History of Company G of the 7th Minnesota Volunteers, War of the Rebellion, 1862–1865," July 23, 1863. MSS 20559. SHSND.

9. Ibid.

10. George C. Pettie diary, July 22, 1863.

11. Eastman diary, July 14, 1863.

12. Smith diary, July 14, 1863.

13. Walter S. Campbell, (pseudonym, Stanley Vestal), "Interviews with White Bull," Collections of Stanley Vestal, boxes 105–106, University of Oklahoma, Norman, Oklahoma.

14. John Pattee, "Reminiscences of John Pattee." *South Dakota Historical Collections* 5: 275–350. Pierre: State Publishing Company, 1910.

15. Kurt D. Bergeman, *Brackett's Battalion* (St. Paul: Minnesota Historical Society Press, 2004), 114.

16. Abner English, "Dakota's First Soldiers," *South Dakota Historical Collections* 9:241–307, Pierre: South Dakota Historical Society, 1918.

17. David Kingsbury, "Sully's Expedition against the Sioux in 1864," *Collections of the Minnesota Historical Society*, vol. 8, St. Paul: Minnesota Historical Society, 1898.

18. Elliott Coues, ed., *History of the Expedition under the Command of Lewis and Clark* (New York: F. P. Harper, 1893), 236.

19. *The North American Journals of Prince Maximilian of Wied, Volume 3, September 1833– August 1834*, edited by Stephen S. Witte and Marsha V. Gallagher, translated by Dieter Karch, foreword by Jack F. Becker, and introduction by Marsh V. Gallagher. University of Oklahoma Press, Norman, in cooperation with the Durham Center for Western Studies, Joslyn Art Museum, Omaha, NE, 2012, 68.

20. Clay S. Jenkinson, ed., *A Vast and Open Plain: The Writings of the Lewis and Clark Expedition in North Dakota, 1804–1806* (Bismarck: State Historical Society of North Dakota, 2003), 108.

21. Alfred W. Bowers, *Hidatsa Social and Ceremonial Organization, Smithsonian Institution, Bureau of American Ethnology*, Bulletin 194 (Washington: Government Printing Office, 1965), 337, footnote 69.

22. "Veteran's Letter Uncovers More Whitestone History," *Dickey County Leader*, June 15, 1950.

23. Kimball Banks, Byron Olson, Dakota Goodhouse, Aaron Barth, and Lorna Meidinger, "Whitestone Hill," *National Register of Historic Places Registration Form* (2013), 32.

More Places to Visit!

ADAMS COUNTY

Dakota Buttes Historical Society
400 S. 11th St.
Hettinger, ND 58639
Museum. History, agriculture, military, textiles.
Historic schoolhouse, restrooms, guided tours
to the area of the Last Great Buffalo Hunt.
GPS 45.95939, -102.86036

BARNES COUNTY

**Barnes County
Historical Society Museum**
315 Central Ave. N.
Valley City, ND 58072-0661
History museum. Museum store, ADA rest-
rooms, guided tours on request.
GPS N 46.92542, -98.00312

Litchville Community Museum
5th St.
Litchville, ND 58461
GPS 46.65368, -98.19138

Rosebud Visitor Center
250 W. Main St.
Valley City, ND 58072
Interpretive Center. History, agriculture, transportation. 1881 railroad superintendent's car,
guided tours, ADA restrooms.
GPS 46.92340, -98.00538

Wimbledon Community Museum, Inc.
401 Railway St.
Wimbledon, ND 58492
Local history museum. National Register build-
ing, agriculture history.
GPS 47.168154, -98.458546

BENSON COUNTY

**Lake Region Pioneer Daughters Museum
at Fort Totten State Historic Site**
817 7th St. N.E.
Devils Lake, ND 58301-2634
History museum. Historic building and
museum store.
GPS 48.1148247, -98.854004

Minnewaukan Historical Society
210 C. Ave.
Minnewaukan ND 58351-0183
Local history museum. National Register build-
ing, guided tours.
GPS 48.06982, -99.24790

BILLINGS COUNTY

Billings County Historical Society Museum
475 4th St.
Medora, ND
Local history museum. National Register
building.
GPS 46.91476, -103.52305

North Dakota Cowboy Hall of Fame
250 Main St.
PO Box 137
Medora, ND 58645
www.northdakotacowboy.com
Fee, museum store, ADA restrooms.
GPS 46.91386, -103.52608

BOTTINEAU COUNTY

Bottineau County Museum
North end of Main St., across from fairgrounds.
Local history museum. Agriculture, toys, cars.
Guided tours available, restrooms.
GPS 48.82785, -100.44594

BOWMAN COUNTY

Pioneer Trails Regional Museum
12 1st Ave N.E.
Bowman, ND 58623
http://www.ptrm.org/
Museum. History, art, geology, paleontology,
archaeology, agriculture, toys, nature. Guided
tours, museum store, reconstructed sod house.
GPS 46.18232, -103.39349

BURKE COUNTY

Burke County Historical Society
Powers Lake, ND 58773
GPS 48.56280, -102.64795

BURLEIGH COUNTY

Buckstop Junction
Missouri Valley Historical Society
3805 E. Bismarck Expressway
Bismarck, ND 58502-0941
http://www.buckstopjunction.org/
Local history museum and interpretive center.
National Register building, historic buildings,
guided tours, museum store, restrooms.
GPS 46.80772, -100.72617

CASS COUNTY

Bonanzaville
Cass County Historical Society
1351 W. Main Ave.
West Fargo, ND 58078
www.bonanzaville.com
GPS 46.87589, -96.92793

Buffalo Heritage Center
204–206 Wilcox Ave.
Buffalo, ND 58011-4115
Museum, historic site.
GPS 46.91969, -97.54953

Fargo Air Museum
1609 19th Ave. N.
Fargo, ND 58102
http://www.fargoairmuseum.org/
Museum and interpretive center. Aviation, military history. Historic Warbird aircraft, aviation
and military research library, active restoration
area. Guided tours, museum store, restrooms,
picnicking.
GPS 46.90538, -96.80408

CAVALIER COUNTY

Cavalier County Historical Society
Dresden, ND
Local history museum.
http://museumatdresden.wordpress.com
GPS 48.825185, -98.482355

DICKEY COUNTY

Dickey County Historical Society
5th and Main
Oakes, ND 58474
GPS 46.138769, -98.093429

Ellendale Historical Society, Inc.
Ellendale, ND 58436
Local history museum. Historic building, guided tours, restrooms.
GPS 46.001474, -98.528599

Fullerton Community Carroll House Historic Hotel and the Rosebud School Museum
19 Monroe St.
Fullerton, ND 58441
GPS 46.16524, -98.42704

DIVIDE COUNTY

Divide County Historical Society and Crosby Museum
210 5th Ave. S.W.
Crosby, ND 58730
Local history museum. Historic and reconstructed buildings, tours by appointment, campground.
GPS 48.91419, -103.29490

DUNN COUNTY

Dunn County Historical Society
153 Museum Trail
Dunn Center, ND 58626
http://www.dunncountymuseum.org/
Local history museum. ADA restrooms.
GPS 47.35477, -102.62313

EDDY COUNTY

Eddy County Museum and Historical Society
1115 1st Ave. N.
New Rockford ND 58356-1701
GPS 47.68114, -99.144005

Sheyenne Log Cabin Museum
Sheyenne, ND 58374
GPS 47.826129, - 99.118813

EMMONS COUNTY

Emmons County Historical Society
110 W. Oak Ave.
Linton, ND 58552
Local history museum. Art, agriculture, toys.
Historic building, guided tours, ADA restrooms.
GPS 46.26992, -100.23439

Hazelton Historical Society
346 Main St.
Hazelton, ND 58544
Local history museum. Historic building, guided tours by appointment.
GPS 46.48474, -100.27738

192 ‹ **More Places To Visit**

FOSTER COUNTY

**Foster County Historical Society
and Putnam House Museum**
Carrington, ND 58421
http://www.putnamhouse.org/
GPS 47.44955, -99.11940

GOLDEN VALLEY COUNTY

Golden Valley County Historical Society
185 1st Ave. S.E.
Beach, ND 58621
Local history museum. History, art, geology,
agriculture, nature. Historic building, guided
tours, restrooms.
GPS 46.91199, -104.00494

GRAND FORKS COUNTY

**Grand Forks County Historical Society
Myra Museum**
2405 Belmont Rd.
Grand Forks, ND 58201
http://grandforkshistory.com/
History museum. National Register building,
historic buildings, guided tours, museum store,
restrooms.
GPS 47.89646, -97.02715

**Larimore Community Museum
and Historical Society**
Larimore, ND 58251
GPS 47.90665, -97.62675

Niagara Community Historical Society
Niagara, ND 58266
GPS 47.99638, -97.87037

**Northwood Pioneer Museum
and Historical Association**
502 Washington St.
Northwood ND 58267-9308
GPS 47.73454, -97.56807

GRANT COUNTY

Grant County Historical Society
Carson, ND 58529
GPS 46.417406, -101.568148

New Leipzig Museum
27 Main Ave. S.
New Leipzig, ND 58562
Local history museum. Agriculture, toys.
Guided tours.
GPS 46.37462, -101.94829

GRIGGS COUNTY

Griggs County Historical Society
203 12th St.
Cooperstown, ND 58425-0242
http://www.griggscountyhistoricalsociety.com/
GPS 47.44249, -98.119208

HETTINGER COUNTY

Mott Gallery of History and Art
Mott Drugstore, Brown Ave.
Mott, ND 58646
GPS 46.37250, -102.32710

KIDDER COUNTY

Kidder County Historical Museum
103 W. Broadway
Steele, ND 58482
GPS 46.85467, -99.91575

LAMOURE COUNTY

LaMoure County Museum
LaMoure, ND 58458
GPS 46.35719, -98.29454

Toy Farmer Museum
LaMoure, ND 58458-9404
http://www.toyfarmer.com/museum/index.html
GPS 46.32659, -98.20212

LOGAN COUNTY

Logan County Historical Society
Napoleon, ND 58561-7217
Local history museum. Agriculture, old store,
school, church, blacksmith shop, newspaper
office, first wooden house in Logan County.
Guided tours, restrooms.
GPS 46.50231, -99.76307

MCHENRY COUNTY

McHenry County Historical Society
Towner, ND 58788-3100
GPS 48.34583, -100.40541

MCINTOSH COUNTY

McIntosh County Historical Society Museum
Ashley, ND 58413
GPS 46.05393, -99.37133

MCKENZIE COUNTY

McKenzie County Museum
Grassy Butte, ND 58634-0116
GPS 47.39251, -103.24796

Lewis and Clark Trail Museum
102 Indiana Ave. E.
Alexander ND 58831
http://www.alexandermuseum.com/
GPS 47.84507, -103.64474

MCLEAN COUNTY

McLean County Historical Society
602 Main Ave.
Washburn, ND 58577-0124
http://www.wrtc.com/vmerkel
/McLeanCountyMuseum/
Local history, art.
GPS 47.2893, -101.08967

Garrison Heritage Park Foundation
241 5th Ave. N.E.
Garrison, ND 58540
Local history museum. Historic building,
guided tours by appointment, restrooms,
picnicking.
GPS 47.65653, -101.41371

MERCER COUNTY

Mercer County Museum
108 7th St.
Beulah, ND 58523
Local history museum. Open Memorial Day
through Labor Day, 1:00–4:00 or by appointment. Guided tours, museum store, ADA
restrooms.
GPS 47.27026, -101.77784

Pfenning Wildlife Museum
1313 Hwy. 49 N.
Beulah, ND 58523
GPS 47.26334, -101.77794

Pioneer Museum of McKenzie County
Watford City, ND 58854
pioneer@ruggedwest.com
GPS 47.799731, -103.283114

North Dakota State Railroad Museum
3102 37th St. N.W.
Mandan, ND 58554
GPS 46.85889, -100.93217

MORTON COUNTY

Almont Historical Society
Almont, ND 58520
Museum. Local history and geology. Historic
building, guided tours by request, ADA restrooms.
GPS 46.72527, -101.50264

Glen Ullin Museum
207 S. 10th St.
Glen Ullin, ND 58631
History museum. Historic buildings, guided
tours, ADA restrooms.
GPS 46.81500, -101.82987

Hebron Historical and Arts Society
Lincoln Ave.
Hebron, ND 58638-0123
Local history museum. Also art, agriculture,
Fort Sauerkraut. Historic building, recon-
structed structures, overlook, guided tours,
restrooms, picnicking.
GPS 46.90056, -102.04544

Mandan Historical Society
Mandan, ND 58554
www.mandanhistory.org
GPS 46.82580, -100.89430

**New Salem Historical Society/
Custer Trail Museum**
N. 8th St.
New Salem, ND 58563
GPS 46.851196, -101.418529

MOUNTRAIL COUNTY

Mountrail County Historical Society
18 2nd Ave. S.E.
Stanley, ND 58784
GPS 48.31734, -102.38907

Plaza Community Museum
607 Main
Plaza, ND 58771
GPS 48.02584, -101.96100

Flickertail Village Museum
Hwy. 2 E.
Stanley, ND 58784
GPS 48.31724, -102.39045

Three Affiliated Tribes Museum
302 Frontage Rd.
New Town, ND 58763-0147
Museum. History, culture of the Mandan,
Hidatsa and Arikara Nation. Museum store,
restrooms.
GPS 47.98054, -102.57722

NELSON COUNTY

**Stump Lake Village/Nelson County
Historical Society**
1044 32nd St. N.E.
Pekin, ND 58361
www.stumplakepark.com
Local history museum. Historic buildings,
guided tours, museum store, restrooms.
Picnicking and camping at Stump Lake Park.
GPS 47.79083, -98.32815

OLIVER COUNTY

Oliver County Historical Society
119 S. Lakota Ave.
Center, ND 58530
GPS 47.11638, -101.29959

PEMBINA COUNTY

Pembina County Historical Society
13572 Hwy. 5
Cavalier, ND 58220
www.ndpchs.com/museum
Local history museum. Also art, agriculture, historic buildings, reconstructed buildings, guided tours, museum store, ADA restrooms.
GPS 48.77276, -97.73506

Blessing Museum
Ox Cart Trails Historical Society
201 Almeron Ave.
Drayton, ND 58225
Local history. Historic building, reconstructed structures, guided tours, museum store.
GPS 48.56171, -97.17968

PIERCE COUNTY

Geographical Center Historical Society
102 Hwy. 2 S.E.
Rugby, ND 58368
www.prairievillagemuseum.com
Museum and interpretive center. History, agriculture, art, toys. Historic buildings, reconstructed structures, museum store, ADA restrooms, picnicking.
GPS 48.37114, -100.00070

RAMSEY COUNTY

Lake Region Heritage Center
(Old Post Office Museum)
502 4th St. N.E.
Devils Lake, ND 58301-0245
www.lakeregionheritagecenter.org/
Museum and Interpretive Center. History, art, geology, culture (American Indian as well as other area cultures). National Register building, guided tours, museum store, restrooms.
GPS 48.11175, -98.85879

Heritage House Museum (Old Sheriff's House)
416 6th St.
P. O. Box 245
Devils Lake, ND 58301
Local history museum. History, toys. National Register building, guided tours, restrooms.
GPS 48.10371, -98.86025

Edmore Historical Society
Edmore, ND 58330
GPS 48.41333, -98.45427

Finnish American Museum,
Pioneer Square Community Center
102 2nd Ave. N.
Brocket, ND 58321-0173
Local history museum. Historic building, restrooms.
GPS 48.21305, -98.35704

RANSOM COUNTY

Ransom County Historical Society
101 Mill Rd.
Fort Ransom, ND 58033-0005
History museum. National Register building, historic buildings.
http://rchsmuseum.tripod.com/
GPS 46.52080, -97.92621

**Bjone Visitor Center and
The Sunne Demonstration Farm**
At Fort Ransom State Park
5981 Walt Hjelle Pkwy.
Fort Ransom, ND 58027
Interpretive Center and Historic Farm. History,
agriculture, nature, historic buildings, reconstructed buildings, guided tours, restrooms,
scenic overlook, picnicking, camping, interpretive programs and demonstrations.
GPS 46.54420, -97.92555

Enderlin Historical Society and Museum
315 Railway
Enderlin, ND 58027
http://enderlinnd.com/HistoricalSociety.aspx
GPS 46.62302, -97.60148

VVVVVVVVVVVVVVVVVVV

RENVILLE COUNTY

Renville County Historical Society
504 1st St. N.E.
Mohall, ND 58761
Local history museum. Historic buildings. ADA
restrooms. Open Sunday afternoons from first
Sunday in June to the last Sunday in August
and by appointment other times.
GPS 48.764444, -101.50529

VVVVVVVVVVVVVVVVVVV

RICHLAND COUNTY

Richland County Historical Society
11 7th Ave. N.
Wahpeton, ND 58075
History, art (pottery), agriculture, Indian arti-
facts, school, museum store, ADA restrooms,
close to park. Guided tours by appointment.
Open Tues, Thurs, Sat. Sun 1–4
GPS 46.27004, -96.60054

**Bagg Bonanza Farm
Historic Preservation Society**
169th Ave. S.E.
Mooreton, ND 58075
1 mile west of I-29 on Hwy 13.
Historic farm museum. Agricultural history,
National Register buildings, National Historic
Landmark, reconstructed structures, guided
tours, museum store, restrooms, picnicking.
GPS 46.23486, -96.86584

Lidgerwood Community Museum
10 3rd Ave. S.E.
Lidgerwood, ND 58053
Museum. History, art, agriculture, toys, nature.
National Landmark, historic building, guided
tours, museum store, restrooms.
GPS 46.075404, -97.147593

VVVVVVVVVVVVVVVVVVV

ROLETTE COUNTY

Rolette County Historical Society
119 6th Ave. N.E.
St. John, ND 58369
GPS 48.94445, -99.71097

Dale and Martha Hawk Museum
Wolford, ND 58385
www.hawkmuseum.org
GPS 48.49860, -99.70430

Turtle Mountain Chippewa Heritage Center
Belcourt, ND 58316
http://chippewa.utma.com/
Museum. History and art. Museum store.
GPS 48.82058, -99.79412

More Places To Visit ➤ 197

SARGENT COUNTY

Sargent County Museum
8987 Hwy. 32
Forman, ND
GPS 46.10774, -97.63648

SHERIDAN COUNTY

**Pioneer Historical Society
for Sheridan County**
609 Frank St. W.
Goodrich ND 58444
GPS 47.47983, -100.12805

SLOPE COUNTY

Unique Antique Auto Museum
305 1st St. W.
Marmarth, ND 58643
Museum. History, Toys, Antique Cars. Museum store, ice cream parlor, restrooms, picnicking.
http://www.marmarth.org/carmuseum
GPS 46.29449, -103.92475

Marmarth Historical Society
P. O. Box 93
Marmarth, ND 58643
GPS 46.29500, -103.92076

STARK COUNTY

Dickinson Museum Center
188 E. Museum Dr., Dickinson, ND 58601-0146
www.dickinsonmuseumcenter.org
History, art, science, agriculture. Historic buildings, reconstructed structures, museum store, guided tours, ADA restrooms, picnicking.
GPS 46.89438, -102.78345

Dakota Dinosaur Museum
200 E. Museum Dr.
Dickinson, ND 58601
www.dakotadino.com
Museum. Geology and paleontology. Museum store, restrooms.
GPS 46.89438, -102.78334

Ukranian Cultural Institute
1221 Villard St. W.
Dickinson, ND 58601
http://www.ukrainianculturalinstitute.org/
Interpretive Center. History, folk arts, performances, ethnic food. Guided tours, museum store, restrooms.
GPS 46.87911, -102.80315

STEELE COUNTY

Steele County Museum
Baldwin's Arcade
Steele Ave. and 3rd St.
Hope, ND 58046
Local history museum. History, art, agriculture, toys, pioneer skills taught, National Register building, historic buildings, guided tours available, museum store, restrooms, picnicking.
GPS 47.32221, -97.72231

STUTSMAN COUNTY

Stutsman County Memorial Museum
321 3rd Ave. S.E.
Jamestown, ND 58401
GPS 46.90611, -98.70533

National Buffalo Museum
500 17th St. S.E.
Jamestown ND 58402-1712
www.buffalomuseum.com
History museum. ADA restrooms, museum
store.
GPS 46.88832, -98.70129

Fort Seward Interpretive Center
602 10th Ave. N.W.
Jamestown, ND 58401
History museum. Guided tours, museum store,
restrooms, picnicking.
GPS 46.91362, -98.72105

TOWNER COUNTY

Towner County Historical Society Museum
Main St.
Egeland, ND
Local history museum. ADA restrooms.
GPS 48.67021, -98.83853

Cando Pioneer Foundation and Museum
502 Main St.
Cando, ND 58324
Local history museum. Historic building,
guided tours.
GPS 48.48986, -99.20361

TRAILL COUNTY

Traill County Historical Society
306 W. Caledonia
Hillsboro, ND 58045-0173
Museum. History, art, agriculture, toys, American Indian artifacts, country schoolhouse,
country church. National Register building,
reconstructed structures, guided tours summer
weekends or by appointment, museum store,
restrooms, picnicking.
GPS 47.40371, -97.05663

Goose River Heritage Center, Inc.
Mayville, ND 58257
History Museum. National Register building,
restrooms.
GPS 47.50021, -97.33195

**Hatton-Eielson Museum
and Historical Association**
405 Eielson St.
Hatton, ND 58240
http://www.eielson.org/
GPS 47.63970, -97.45342

WALSH COUNTY

Walsh County Historical Society
323 3rd St.
Minto, ND 58261
Local history museum, agriculture, toys, historic building, restrooms.
GPS 48.29340, -97.37303

More Places To Visit ➤ **199**

Heritage Village at Grafton
625 W. 12th
Grafton, ND 58237
Local history museum. Historic and reconstructed buildings, agriculture, toys, nature, tours by request, restrooms. Carousel rides. Open Sundays in the summer from 1-5.
GPS 48.41250, -97.42044

WARD COUNTY

Ward County Historical Museum
Minot, ND 58702
http://www.wchsnd.org/
Local history museum. Historical buildings, reconstructed buildings. Agriculture and transportation. Guided tours by appointment, restrooms.
GPS 48.22300, -101.32143

Railroad Museum of Minot
19 1st St. N.E.
Minot, ND 58701
http://railroadmuseumofminot.com/
GPS 48.23704, -101.29169

Dakota Territory Air Museum
100 34th Ave. N.E.
Minot, ND 58701
http://dakotaterritoryairmuseum.com/
History. Historical aircraft, aviation research library, fire trucks, guided tours, museum store, restrooms.
GPS 48.27248, -101.29034

Lake County Historical Society
Hwy. 52
Kenmare, ND 58746
Local history museum. Pioneer and military history in twenty buildings, guided tours, restrooms. Open Memorial Day through Labor Day Wednesday through Sunday or by appointment.
GPS 48.67384, -102.06853

Ryder Historical Society and Museum
SE Main St.
Ryder, ND 58779
History museum. Historic building, tours by request, ADA restrooms. Open June through August on Wednesdays from 10:00 A.M. to 4:00 P.M.
GPS 47.91750, -101.67794

WELLS COUNTY

Wells County Historical Museum
Fairgrounds
Fessenden, ND 58438
Local history museum. Historic building.
GPS 47.64916, -99.62928

Bowdon Museum and Library
419 Chester Ave. W.
Bowdon, ND 58418
GPS 47.46972, -99.70789

Manfred Heritage Museum
130 Lake Ave.
Manfred, ND
www.manfrednd.org/
Local history museum. Historical buildings, agriculture, nature, flowers, picnicking, reconstructed structures, museum store, guided tours, hands-on activities.
GPS 47.69408, -99.74781

WILLIAMS COUNTY

Buffalo Trails Museum
203 Main St.
Epping, ND 58843
Local history museum. Art, geology, agriculture, toys, nature, homesteader items in eight buildings.
GPS 48.27987, -103.35816

Frontier Museum
6330 2nd Ave. W.
Williston, ND 58801
GPS 48.14765, -103.62353

Pioneer Trails Museum
Hanks, ND
Local history museum, agriculture. Historic building, guided tours, restrooms.
GPS 48.60675, -103.80020

Ray Opera House Museum Society
Ray, ND 58849-0023
History museum, art, toys. Historic building, ADA restrooms.
GPS 48.34664, -103.15834

Tioga Historical Society
Norseman Museum
17 2nd St. N.E.
Tioga, ND 58852
GPS 48.39724, -102.93823

Index by Theme

NATURAL HISTORY

Cross Ranch State Park 30

Fort Buford and the Missouri Yellowstone Confluence Interpretive Center 53

Fort Stevenson State Park 73

Icelandic State Park 92

International Peace Garden 95

Knife River Indian Villages National Historic Site 102

Theodore Roosevelt National Park 149

Turtle River State Park 156

NATIVE AMERICAN

Big Mound State Historic Site 6

Cross Ranch State Park 30

Crowley Flint Quarry State Historic Site 32

Double Ditch Indian Village State Historic Site 40

Fort Abraham Lincoln State Park 50

Fort Clark Trading Post State Historic Site 57

Fort Totten State Historic Site 76

Fort Union Trading Post National Historic Site 81

Huff Indian Village State Historic Site 89

Killdeer Mountain Battlefield State Historic Site 98

Knife River Indian Villages National Historic Site 102

McPhail's Butte Overlook State Historic Site 110

Medicine Rock State Historic Site 111

Menoken Indian Village State Historic Site 113

Molander Indian Village State Historic Site 115

Pulver Mounds State Historic Site 130

Sitting Bull Burial 137

Standing Rock State Historic Site 140

Turtle Effigy State Historic Site 154

Whitestone Hill State Historic Site 164

Writing Rock State Historic Site 169

EXPLORATION AND SETTLEMENT

Brenner Crossing State Historic Site 12

David Thompson State Historic Site 34

De Morés State Historic Site 36

Fort Abercrombie State Historic Site 47

Fort Mandan Overlook State Historic Site 65

Hudson Townsite State Historic Site 87

Icelandic State Park 92

Lake Jessie State Historic Site 105

North Dakota Lewis and Clark Interpretive Center and Fort Mandan 121

Oak Lawn Church State Historic Site 125

St. Claude State Historic Site 136

Sully's Heart River Corral State Historic Site 146

Sweden State Historic Site 148

Theodore Roosevelt National Park 149

Wadeson Cabin State Historic Site 159

Walhalla State Historic Site 160

Welk Homestead 162

MILITARY

Big Mound State Historic Site 6
Buffalo Creek State Historic Site 13
Camp Arnold State Historic Site 14
Camp Atchison State Historic Site 15
Camp Buell State Historic Site 18
Camp Corning State Historic Site 19
Camp Grant State Historic Site 20
Camp Hancock State Historic Site 21
Camp Kimball State Historic Site 24
Camp Sheardown State Historic Site 25
Camp Weiser State Historic Site 26
Camp Whitney State Historic Site 27
Fort Abercrombie State Historic Site 47
Fort Abraham Lincoln State Park 50
Fort Buford and the Missouri Yellowstone Confluence Interpretive Center 53
Fort Dilts State Historic Site 62
Fort Ransom State Historic Site 67
Fort Rice State Historic Site 69
Fort Stevenson State Park 73
Fort Totten State Historic Site 76
Killdeer Mountain Battlefield State Historic Site 98
Lake Johnson State Historic Site 106
McPhail's Butte Overlook State Historic Site 110
Palmer's Spring State Historic Site 126
Ronald Reagan Miniuteman Missile State Historic Site 132
Sully's Heart River Corral State Historic Site 146
Whitestone Hill State Historic Site 164

TRADE AND TECHNOLOGY

Bismarck Deadwood Stage Trail State Historic Site 10
Camp Hancock State Historic Site 21
Cannonball Stage Station State Historic Site 28
Crowley Flint Quarry State Historic Site 32
De Morés State Historic Site 36
Double Ditch Indian Village State Historic Site 40
Fort Clark Trading Post State Historic Site 57
Fort Union Trading Post National Historic Site 81
Gingras Trading Post State Historic Site 85
Maple Creek Crossing State Historic Site 108
Steamboat Warehouse State Historic Site 142
Walhalla State Historic Site 160

GOVERNMENT

Camp Hancock State Historic Site 21
Former Governors' Mansion State Historic Site 44
Stutsman County Courthouse State Historic Site 144

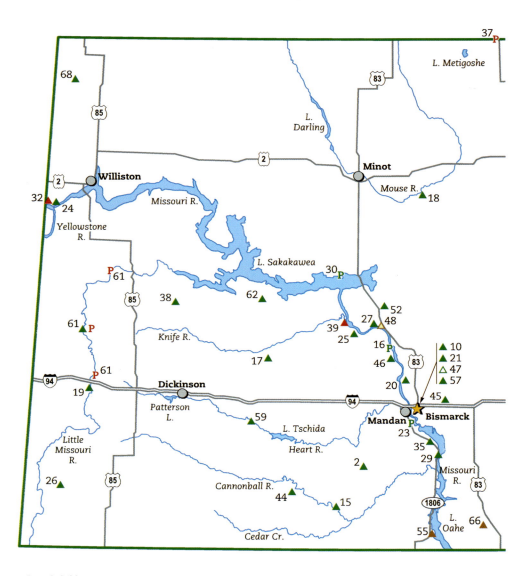

1. Big Mound Battlefield
2. Bismarck-Deadwood Stage Trail
3. Brenner Crossing
4. Buffalo Creek
5. Camp Arnold
6. Camp Atchison
7. CampBuell
8. Camp Corning
9. Camp Grant
10. Camp Hancock
11. Camp Kimball
12. Camp Sheardown
13. Camp Weiser
14. Camp Whitney
15. Cannonball Stage Station
16. Cross Ranch SP
17. Crowley Flint Quarry
18. David Thompson
19. De Mores
20. Double Ditch Indian Village
21. Former Governors' Mansion
22. Fort Abercrombie
23. Fort Abraham Lincoln SP
24. Fort Buford & Missouri-Yellowstone Confluence Interpretive Center
25. Fort Clark Trading Post
26. Fort Dilts
27. Fort Mandan Overlook
28. Fort Ransom
29. Fort Rice
30. Fort Stevenson SP
31. Fort Totten
32. Fort Union Trading Post NHS
33. Gingras Trading Post
34. Hudson Townsite
35. Huff Indian Village
36. Icelandic SP
37. International Peace Garden
38. Killdeer Mountain Battlefield

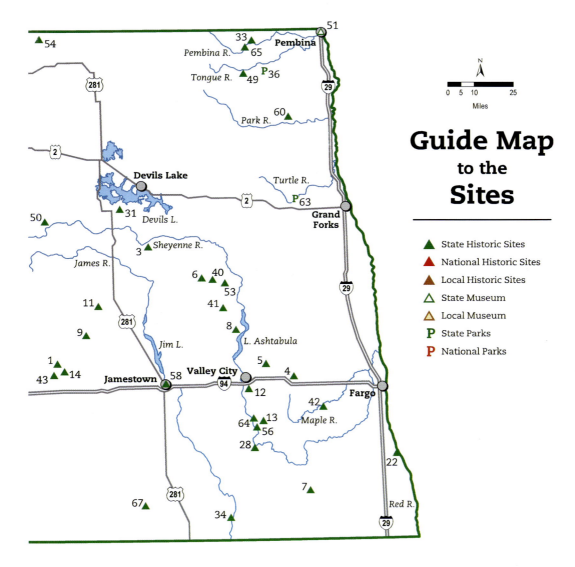

39. Knife River Indian Villages NHS
40. Lake Jessie
41. Lake Johnson
42. Maple Creek Crossing
43. McPhail's Butte
44. Medicine Rock
45. Menoken Indian Village
46. Molander Indian Village
47. North Dakota Heritage Center
48. North Dakota Lewis & Clark Interpretive Center
49. Oak Lawn
50. Palmer's Spring
51. Pembina State Museum
52. Pulver Mounds
53. Ronald Reagan Minuteman Missile
54. St. Claude
55. Sitting Bull Burial
56. Standing Rock
57. Steamboat Warehouse
58. Stutsman County Courthouse
59. Sully's Heart River Corral
60. Sweden
61. Theodore Roosevelt NP
62. Turtle Effigy
63. Turtle River SP
64. Wadeson Cabin
65. Walhalla
66. Welk Homestead
67. Whitestone Hill
68. Writing Rock

There are a variety of routes one can take from Medora south to Bowman and Fort Dilts State Historic Site, as illustrated by a map available at the de Morés Interpretive Center (page 38). Following the southern route, 13 miles west and north of Amidon, North Dakota, along the picturesque East River Road, a stop at the Burning Coal Vein is a pleasant detour. Traveling 1.7 miles east of East River, a gravel road brings the visitor to a parking area overlooking this sandstone tower and the unusual trees this site is known for. Likely started long ago by a lightning strike, a burning coal vein still occasionally emits gasses. Downwind gasses from the fire change the growth of normally round Rocky Mountain Juniper trees to a columnar variety. Unmarked hiking trails and a campground make this site one for the modern explorer's "must-do" list.